ALSO BY MARGOT FONTEYN

A Dancer's World

Autobiography

THESE ARE BORZOI BOOKS, PUBLISHED IN NEW YORK BY ALFRED A. KNOPF.

THE MAGIC OF DANCE

THE MAGIC OF DANCE

MARGOT FONTEYN

ALFRED A. KNOPF
NEW YORK
1979

THIS IS A BORZOI BOOK

PUBLISHED BY ALFRED A. KNOPF, INC.

Library of Congress Cataloging in Publication Data
Fonteyn, Margot, Dame (date) / The magic of dance.
Includes index.
1. Dancing—History.   2. Ballet—History.   I. Title.
GV1617.F66   1979   793.3'09   79-2221
ISBN 0-394-50778-9
Manufactured in the United States of America
First American Edition

THE MAGIC OF DANCE

ACKNOWLEDGMENTS

I wish to give thanks first to the British Broadcasting Corporation and Aubrey Singer for accepting my idea for *The Magic of Dance* television programs, which brought this book into existence; to the B.B.C. producer, Patricia Foy, for her tremendous patience and help during its preparation; to Robert Gottlieb, of Alfred A. Knopf, Inc., for being lenient, demanding, critical, encouraging and passionately involved in every detail of the book; and to inspired researcher, Catherine Ashmore, for the three years of tireless bloodhounding for the illustrations.

Other people who have helped me in a variety of ways are Dame Marie Rambert; Sir Frederick Ashton; Professor Rikki Raab; Martha Graham; Gunhild Schüller; Boris Oberzaucher; Parmenia Migel; Bengt Häger; Ivor Guest; Nigel Gosling; Hands Bundy and Suzanne Kirnbauer; Rudolf Nureyev; Anna Duncan; Therese Duncan; Henning Kronstam; Ivan Nagy; Mary Skeaping; Joy Brown; Vincenzo Celli; Joseph Stuhl; John Lazzarini; Trader Faulkner; Lennart Rudling; Richard C. Shultz; the late Derra de Moroda; the late Giovanni Poli; and my brother, Felix Fonteyn, who, among other things, thought of the title.

My thanks, also, to those at Knopf who have worked so hard on this book: to Bob Scudellari and Sara Eisenman, who are responsible for the design; to Ellen McNeilly, who oversaw the production; and to Neal Jones and Nancy Clements, production editors.

Finally, my appreciation, inexpressible, goes to Gillian Branston and Karen Latuchie for transformations, magical, to my manuscripts—undecipherable.

Margot Fonteyn

THE MAGIC OF DANCE

DANCE MAGICAL

There has always been magic in dance, but in such variety and in so many places at different times that it is hard to know where to start talking about it. I am far too contrary by nature to begin at the beginning and work forward chronologically. The very idea is tedious, and even if it were not, who knows for sure how or where dance began? In any case, this book is *not* a history—if it were there would be many omissions. *The Magic of Dance* contains my own understanding of people and influences, and of patterns that can be observed repeating themselves—from which, maybe, one can get a hint of what might come in the future.

The story concerns people more than anything else. People can be magical and theatre can be magical, so, of necessity, most of the story is about the important personalities of dance in the theatre. Some of them are famous, some forgotten, but all in their time and place had magic.

Since I am the one regarding this scene, I find it easier to start from what I have observed during the span of my career and then go back to the causes leading to those events, before looking back further to see what produced the causes and so on. Within each chapter I look at the scene more or less chronologically, and in the last part I come back to the present and possible future—I am sure that some other female minds will find this system as clear and logical as I do.

The fortuitous circumstance that *The Magic of Dance* was conceived simultaneously as a book and as a B.B.C. television series has given me the added adventure of exploration that the book alone would have denied me. Literary research can be done from an armchair, but the excitement of film is to show places associated with legendary people and events, and to be with those who are legends now in their lifetime. Fred Astaire, for example, is one of the great dancers of all time. His films are re-run constantly but it is rare to be accorded a personal interview and delightful to savour his total lack of awareness that

WITH FRED ASTAIRE   IN PAVLOVA'S LONDON HOME, IVY HOUSE

his genius helped to pave the way for today's supreme male ballet stars and the consequent boom in dance of all kinds.

People influencing dance have been of two kinds: those who advanced the art by contributing to its evolution one way or another and those who spread the knowledge. Fred Astaire had both kinds of influence: he restored respect for the male dancer, and the demand for his films reached, and continue to enchant, millions around the world.

The process of converting some of my ideas into visual stories for the television series increased my knowledge and understanding of the subject far more than I had expected. I did not know when I started that there is a house—at present in ruins—on an Athenian hilltop where Isadora Duncan lived for a time and intended, with the addition of a Greek temple and amphitheatre, to re-create the life style of antiquity. I knew she went to the Parthenon to seek inspiration, but I could never have imagined the surpassing beauty of the temple as I experienced it standing alone among the columns at dawn.

In another, colder dawn I was entranced by the Chinese Tai-Chi exercises, one thousand years old, yet surprisingly like modern dance, as practised by mostly middle-aged citizens of Shanghai on the Bund—the city waterfront from where I sailed to England to try my chances in ballet when I was fourteen.

There is an eighteenth-century theatre in Sweden that was somehow closed and forgotten for over one hundred years. I knew of its existence, but I did not expect the amazing ingenuity and efficiency of its stage mechanisms that can make complete scene transformations in ten seconds. Nor did I know of the Farnese Theatre in Parma, which

IN ISADORA DUNCAN'S HOUSE, ATHENS

DESCENDING THE STAGE-TRAP OF DROTTNINGHOLM COURT THEATRE, SWEDEN

has the earliest surviving proscenium stage as well as an arena-like auditorium—nor was I aware of the incredible story of the first performance ever given there.

Anna Pavlova's house in London, one room of which is opened as a museum at weekends, was familiar of course, but, on the trail of places associated with Marie Taglioni (she lived in London for three years towards the end of her life), I learned almost by chance that her grandparents' home outside Stockholm still stands unchanged in a delightful garden full of lilac bushes where she must certainly have walked many times.

Then there was an amazing find while we were filming *Le Spectre de la Rose* in the Monte Carlo Theatre, where it had its première in 1911. There was some difficulty about matching all the furnishings to a photograph of the original production. When it was shown to the property master he went off and rummaged in the back of his storeroom, returning in triumph with a little birdcage and a needlework frame identical to the ones in the picture—and presumably the originals.

I went to Vienna to look for Fanny Elssler's birthplace and found instead a dance performed by Grete Wiesenthal in 1907 and preserved in every detail by one of her pupils. Not only that, but we were able to record it in an art nouveau apartment perfect for the period.

I came across some interesting parallels—that between Juba, a marvellous American

IN SHANGHAI

dancer and singer in the 1840's, and Sammy Davis, Jr., was one of them; and I talked to Vaslav Nijinsky's daughter Kyra. She has his green eyes and heart-warming laugh.

These and many other experiences have made the preparation of this book totally absorbing, and the search for illustrations sometimes resembled a treasure hunt. It was a triumph to find a picture of Marie Taglioni's father, Filippo, who made her into what is now our image of a Romantic ballerina—a figure that did not exist before. She is usually given the credit for what was obviously her father's creation, and for some reason he gets scant attention, so his portrait is very rarely published. Then there are people like Nijinsky, whose photographs are so well known that it is a real scoop to find one not yet seen in other books.

There is unsuspected knowledge to be gleaned from photographs. Nijinsky becomes completely one with the ballet character he is portraying—he has extraordinary abandon in the sweep of his body; but in day clothes he is very straight and serious, never relaxed. Isadora Duncan is surprisingly carefully posed, there is little movement in her pictures. Ruth St. Denis is much the same, but Martha Graham's photographs are full of action forcefully expressing the character of her dance. Pierina Legnani, the first to dance *Swan Lake* in 1895, looks short and dumpy; it is impossible to imagine her in the famous second-act swan pas de deux.

WITH MIKHAIL BARYSHNIKOV IN *LE SPECTRE D*

ROSE, ROYAL OPERA HOUSE, MONTE CARLO

Tamara Karsavina in her photographs is seductive, enchanting, coquettish, demure, innocent, or haughty—she captures every aspect of femininity. She is always a woman. When it comes to Anna Pavlova, there is no limit to the subtlety of her expression; in her swan costume she *is* a swan, in *Oriental Impressions* she *is* Indian, and in ordinary life no fashion model could carry off clothes (especially hats) as she does, nor look just right teaching an elephant to stand in arabesque!

It may seem strange for me to say that during the forty-some years of my career I read very little about dance; the activity itself was totally absorbing. I knew the general history from my student days, but I had no desire to delve more deeply until those years of experience on the stage began to press on my mind and odd questions would crop up. When Pavlova died she was just over fifty; I wondered whether she wanted to retire but felt trapped by an obligation to keep her dancers employed. I wondered about the rise of ballet in Russia: why did it happen so far from the artistic centre of Europe?

As I looked for answers, I came to sense, rightly or wrongly, that I have a "back-stage" understanding of many of the people and how they felt in certain situations. Fanny Elssler described her conquest of New York and her apprehension preceding the première. I've lived through the same experience, I know the ensnaring attraction of rehearsal rooms and dressing rooms, and the menace of that dark area beyond the footlights as the heavy curtain rises and the muffled overture gives way to the ballet's opening bars. The music wells up loud and clear, the show is starting, the dread moment is here—this is it! And I know the triumph one hadn't dared to hope for, the public standing and shouting, the flowers, and—the relief. It worked!

I know the irresistible challenge, the cost of facing it, and the satisfaction of winning. I know the full excitement of success and I know its emptiness. I feel that I've come to know the people in this book: the French ballet masters who went to Russia, John Durang in America, Johann Strauss in Vienna, and Juba, who danced until he wore himself out at the age of twenty-seven and died.

I know now that Anna Pavlova could not have lived without dancing. If she began to find it too great a burden, it was better that she should float gracefully away from this life. In a curious way I believe that is just what happened when, in her fevered delirium, as pleurisy reached its crisis, she asked for her swan costume.

I commend all these people to you, hoping you will read about them and look searchingly into their pictures. Their lives have mostly gone, or are still going, into the making of magic—the magic of dance.

IN THE HALL OF MIRRORS, PALACE OF VERSAILLES

DANCE UNIVERSAL

It was not just perversity that made me decide to start looking at dance from the span of my own career. This happens to be one of the most interesting—and maybe *the* most interesting—periods in all the long story of dance because of the speed with which so many threads have drawn together. The changes in my little world of dance since I first entered Sadler's Wells Theatre in 1934 have been astounding. The public then was really a tiny minority, and now one can fairly say that dance is universal.

The first thing that strikes me about this change is that it couldn't have happened without the appearance on the scene of male dancers—for there were very few in 1934. That was definitely what I would call "the era of the ballerina," and the greater part of my career took place in the last phases of that era, when no right-minded man was supposed to take up dancing as a profession. This was an extraordinary situation, because dance is very much a man's activity, as a quick look at current stars will prove. Rudolf Nureyev's name is known throughout the world; far beyond the dance public. He changed the face of ballet by setting a completely modern image. Mikhail Baryshnikov is adored by millions of moviegoers (ballet- and nonballet-minded) from one film, *The Turning Point*. So, in his very different dance style, is John Travolta, from *Saturday Night Fever*, but, except for Moira Shearer in *The Red Shoes*, no ballerina has ever caught the mass movie public. Ginger Rogers? Yes, of course, although without Fred Astaire we would not have seen the same Ginger Rogers, and would she have had the same success?

Since, from primitive times, dance was always the concern of men, and at various points in history an accomplishment quite as important socially as wit and good manners—and the requisite of a good soldier too—it is intriguing to surmise how and why women were able to take it over almost completely. What is sure is that this abnormal situation brought about such a deterioration in the ballet of western Europe in the latter part of the nineteenth century that it seemed lost beyond recall. Only in Russia, eastern Europe,

"ERA OF THE BALLERINA"

TAMARA TOUMANOVA   YVETTE CHAUVIRÉ

PAS DE QUATRE, NATALIA KRASSOVSKA, ALICIA MARKOVA,
TATIANA RIABOUCHINSKA, AND ALEXANDRA DANILOVA

OLGA SPESSIVTSEVA

MOIRA SHEARER AND ROBERT HELPMANN IN *THE RED SHOES*

and Denmark did male dancing survive as a serious occupation and, as a consequence, ballet there was still regarded as a serious art.

It is hard to understand why there should have been such a difference between one area and another, and why in Russia the ballet should have reached a high point at precisely the time it was rotting elsewhere. A possible explanation could lie in the effect of the Industrial Revolution on the lives of thousands of men in the countries of western Europe. Russia remained an enormous agricultural area, and since in rural societies wherever there is folk dancing it is the men who excel, the idea of men as dancers did not devalue. In Hungary, and perhaps elsewhere, folk dancing was even used by the army as a means of recruitment. On arriving in a small town or village, the recruiting contingent would begin dancing in the main square and invite the local youths to join in. The best dancers among them were given preference by the enlisting officer because they were likely to be alert and become a credit to the regiment. Today the Red Army Choir and Dancers actually function as a permanent theatre group. Many of their dances, like folk dances all over the

RUSSIAN FOLK DANCE

world, are on the simple theme of impressing the village girls with a show of virile leaps and spins. Other dances are directly related to workaday occupations.

This had been the way of life for centuries and it changed very little prior to the revolution brought about by industrialization, which as it ate up more and more of the countryside forced increasing numbers of light-hearted and light-footed young men out of the fields and into factories. In their new environment, dance went out of their lives. In factories there are no traditional dances handed down from generation to generation, and learned in childhood at celebrations and festivals on the village green. Factory workers

ILLAGE DANCE

have only an occasional Saturday-night social dance, totally lacking any local roots or character. Therefore, the vital force of dance—the compulsion and the enjoyment—became estranged from the ordinary working life of men. Possibly as a consequence, in the theatre, also, dance ceased to be a man's job and became an occupation suitable only for girls. An English critic writing in 1911 made the serious comment that, as a rule, a man would rather be caught in the act of stealing than of dancing! Thus was the age-old order of things reversed: youths no longer danced to impress the girls, now it was the girls who pointed a pretty toe and smiled a sweet smile to attract the best looking—or richest—men.

Another factor that helped to alienate men from an active role in dance was the introduction of waltzing early in the nineteenth century. Quite simply, the waltz thrust women into men's arms and, thus encumbered, the range of their steps was severely limited. Earlier court dances had offered such a variety of interesting footwork that a good dancer in the ballroom was halfway to ballet, but all this was eroded by the waltz, and even before that, by an eighteenth-century dance called the allemande, in which the couples held each other's hands continuously.

Since there is always an element of flirtation in social dance, the waltz won the battle, as it were, before it started, because the gentleman could clasp a girl in his arms without having to master a lot of difficult steps to impress her. That most important objective of his dancing had slipped to second place, and from then on, men's motivation to become dancers went imperceptibly downhill until dancing grew to be considered positively un-

AN EARLY WALTZ

THE ALLEMANDE, C. 1760

WALTZING AT THE GREAT RUSSIAN BALL, NEW YORK, 1863

En travestie: LOUISE FAIRBROTHER AS ABDULLAH, 1848, AND SARAH JANE WOOLGAR AS DUKE ALBERT, 1847

worthy of a man's interest at all.

In these circumstances male ballet dancers were understandably a rarity; instead of being a valued part of the whole ballet structure, as they still were in Russia, they were either maligned or ignored altogether. On occasion they were replaced by girls dressed *en travestie*—to the perfect satisfaction of gentlemen patrons of the opera and music halls. The sight of a pretty girl in knee breeches was tantalizing, whereas a man wearing ballet costume was generally thought to be repugnant.

Obviously there were few candidates for the man's job, but, without them, creativity in the art as a whole plummeted to levels of sugary nonsense. In Degas' scenes of ballet life at the Paris Opera, from the 1860's to the 1880's, there is not a trace of a male dancer to be found, only an occasional ballet master or musician or the top-hatted patrons of the front row courting their favorites. Yet Paris had originally been the very centre and fountain-head of ballet.

Early in the new century there appeared in Paris itself a little hint that the tide in Europe would one day turn, but few cared enough about ballet by then to consider whether there could be any connection between the Opera stage and the short-lived apache dance of the slums. I believe the apache came from the earliest form of cancan—before it was a night-club shocker—and that the cancan in turn came from a form of country dance performed in popular dance halls. The tenuous connection of apache with ballet is that it brought a new impetus; and as usual, the new impetus did not start in the theatre, but travelled up through social dancing, reaching the ballet last of all.

DEGAS' *REHEARSAL OF THE BALLET ON THE STAGE*

THE APACHE

The apache was a genuine folk dance of the industrialized world; it was a city product, and in it the men were definitely dominant, throwing their partners about without any consideration for decorum or dignity. It proved a bit too rough for adaptation to the society ballroom and so went straight to the stage as a popular vaudeville or cabaret number; after a fairly brief life, it just died, without achieving much for the cause of men in dance. Nevertheless, what took its place, and has lived on in music, ballroom, and theatre, is another genuine city folk dance, this time from the docks of Buenos Aires—the tango. It proclaimed man's dominance in no uncertain terms, but, being musically more subtle than the apache, it needed only a generous dose of polish and elegance to make it perfect for the

THE TANGO

ballroom floor, where nothing so revolutionary had appeared since the waltz a hundred years before. The tango called for skill, and men were caught off guard because they hadn't bothered about dance for so long.

This led to a new profession—that of the exhibition dancer; and with the exhibition dancer came a quick succession of new dances, a spate of new rhythms on new phonograph records, new schools of ballroom dance, and that delightful afternoon pastime, the thé dansant. At teatime, husbands were apt to be in the office, so a new necessity arose—the "gigolo," who was a thoroughly professional dancer but suffered the poor image attached to any man who would earn his living in so unworthy an occupation.

However, nothing could now reverse the tremendous boom in ballroom dancing. Right at the centre of it, in the United States, were Vernon Castle and his wife, Irene, superb exhibition dancers who proved that art lies not so much in the type of dance but the manner in which it is performed. Their dancing was beautiful, graceful, and chic, and in his field Vernon Castle was a very able choreographer, devising the Maxixe, the Castle Walk, the Hesitation Waltz, and many other successes.

Instead of being maligned as a male dancer, Castle was greatly admired, and not only by an élite public. Tragically, he was killed while serving in World War I. His popularity with all levels of society had restored some respect to the profession, although it would be a long time yet before that respect extended fully to ballet—not even Vaslav Nijinsky's fame between 1909 and 1916 made much impression, for his image was of a fantastic aerial creature so far removed from ordinary life that he could have come from

IRENE AND VERNON CASTLE AT CASTLE HOUSE

THE CASTLES

THE SILENT DANCE, 1928

another planet. It is unlikely that any self-respecting man in the audience imagined himself as another Nijinsky dancing the Faun or the Spirit of the Rose. But the persuasive music of ragtime was another matter; ragtime—another genuine folk dance of the city—was modern, it was for everyone, and many a male foot unconsciously tapped out its infectious rhythm.

The end of World War I ushered in an optimistic new world and with it, in the 1920's, came the Charleston, that gloriously crazy, happy dance in which men were finally released from the burden of steering their partners around the floor. At last they were free to swing their arms, twist their shoulders, kick their legs, hop and turn, and generally get back to the business of dance in some of its primitive frenzy. It was a turning point for men's liberation on the dance floor. European social dances had been travelling sedately westwards for two centuries before the 1920's. Then the Charleston rushed across the Atlantic in the opposite direction to burst upon Europe like an epidemic of St. Vitus Dance. It travelled first-class, second-class, steerage, and on celluloid via movies; it invaded salons, ballrooms, nightclubs, dance halls, and variety theatres; it was everywhere at once, danced by men, women, and children. To some extent, it was an exultant expression of belief that war had been banished from the world and life was going to be "just a bowl of cherries."

THE CHARLESTON

THE CHARLESTON

1926

LEARNING THE CHARLESTON

BEE JACKSON, WORLD CHARLESTON CHAMPION

FRED AND ADELE ASTAIRE, 1906

From the Charleston it was an easy step to the emergence of a male superstar dancer, and he was ready and waiting at exactly the right moment. He was the great Fred Astaire, with his magic of magic, who made dancing look easier than walking, more natural than breathing, and indisputably masculine. Perhaps no one thought of it at the time, certainly not Fred, but in retrospect it is clear that he, more than anyone else, led men back to their rightful place in the world of dance. His technique, his timing, his style were all impeccable, and when he went to Hollywood in the early thirties, the centre of dance magic suddenly and surprisingly settled in that city. For a while there was nothing so innovative anywhere else in the world as his filmed sequences, with their inventive choreography, slick dancing, and trick camerawork. Although modern dance was in the pioneering stage

THE ASTAIRES

at that time and English ballet was busy formulating its tradition, they were both still in infancy—but dance on the screen reached adulthood with Fred Astaire. That is one of the
most fascinating aspects of Astaire's early films. It would appear that he understood the
new medium instinctively and, from the first day, hit upon the right formula to compensate
for the missing third dimension. Sometimes it would be a question of changing his working level by dancing up a flight of stairs or over the furniture, sometimes just a shift in the
background setting, or he might employ a striking cinematic trick or simply make use of a
prop, like the famous walking stick.

   As an artist brought up from early childhood on the stage, with its fixed dimensions
and its laws governed by the proscenium opening, Fred adapted remarkably quickly to the

screen's total freedom of space and orientation. His biggest asset was his style of dancing, built up laboriously through many years, which masked all difficulties with the most beguiling nonchalance. No one has ever quite matched his perfection on film. Everything came together in those brilliant sequences: the originality, the choreography, the timing, and, above all, the "star" that was the man himself.

How can one describe the art of Fred Astaire? First, I would talk of his ideal proportions: his slender build, long legs, shoulders neither too narrow nor too wide, head neither too large nor too small. It is not often that a dancer is proportioned so harmoniously from head to elegant foot. Sometimes a half inch too little in the length of arm, or too much from forehead to chin, mars the overall appearance. With Astaire the balance is perfect.

Second, I would think of the marvellous relaxation of his movements. Even to see him enter a room is a pleasure because his walk so perfectly expresses the assurance of a great artist tempered by the genuine reticence he feels about his fame. Whether dancing or not, all his movements are infused with a relaxed, easy charm. "Debonair" was a word used in the thirties to describe him, and I think it suits very well. It suggests a person of good disposition, happy, easygoing, and amiable, or "with a good manner of being."

When it comes to defining his star quality, who can ever pinpoint that elusive commodity in any artist? It is different in each case; the public recognizes it but the artist himself has no idea of what it is compounded. Some people think it resides in an irrepressible urge to communicate by way of the chosen art, and some great artists have felt this urge but others not. Fred Astaire was one who, as a child, had no inner drive to dance. His career began because of his sister Adele's obvious talent for the stage, which involved Fred, from force of circumstance, in her early training; and here we come across one of those fascinating stories of theatre life and family sacrifice. Fred's father had left his native Vienna as a young man and settled in Omaha, Nebraska. He had all the easy bonhomie of the Viennese people, and had always loved music, cafés, theatres, and theatre folk. As soon as he saw that his young daughter was an apparently promising little dancer, he and his wife decided she must be taken to New York to give her talent a chance. The extraordinary thing was that this sacrifice was made when Adele was not yet six years old. Father had to remain in Omaha supporting the family, but Fred, who was only four and a half, naturally went with his mother and sister, and since he was too young to be left alone, he was taken along to Adele's dancing classes. In time, and with the help of his sister, who was the greater star of the two until she retired to marry, he became the unique Fred Astaire. It was a long, slow journey.

FRED ASTAIRE AND GINGER ROGERS IN *TOP HAT*, 1935

ASTAIRE AND ROGERS IN *SWING TIME*, 1936

ASTAIRE AND ROGERS IN *CAREFREE*, 1938

If I had to pick one of his virtues as the most important in his rise to the top, I would choose his sense of perfection. It shines through all his work; there is never a trace of effort, and that is because he had devoted infinite patience to rehearsing and perfecting every detail. His technique is astounding, yet everything is accomplished with the air of someone sauntering through the park on a spring morning.

Typically, Fred hates to talk about himself or his art. He cannot theorize about his creations beyond describing how, when embarking on a new number, he tried never to repeat an idea or theme he had used before. He has no explanation for his genius. All he says is, "I just dance!"—and it looks just as simple as that. Yet imagine for a moment that Astaire in the thirties was not dressed in top hat and tails but in tights and slippers, and that his genius was for ballet. What opportunities would he have had then to exploit his art?

Few indeed; it was very definitely the era of the ballerina. It is precisely because Astaire's image was of a man in a lounge suit, a sports shirt, or dress clothes—that is, in the normal attire of people not employed in ballet—that he was able to reinstate men as dancers in the eyes of the general public; and also because his style of dance was based on jazz.

Jazz is part of the genuine folk culture of North America, and the only such national tradition to emerge new in the twentieth century. Consequently it has been an extraordinarily important force in theatre dance—a modern counterpart to the European folk dances that seasoned so much of nineteenth-century ballet, adding rhythm and colour. Jazz itself is a freak case, because the American folklore art should have grown out of a blend of European and indigenous American Indian traditions. Instead, the white settlers left most of their own dances behind in the old countries, and in the New World were understandably

THE BLACK BOTTOM

too busy saving their scalps to worry about preserving and absorbing native culture. The two cultures remained quite separate, and consequently, while the white people gradually lost their European identities and became Americans, their folklore—country music and square dancing—remained essentially European, without genuine roots in their new land. Nothing developed that can be compared to the lively music and dance of all Latin America, where the conquistadores intermingled their own Iberian dances with local Indian cultures so successfully. This cross-breeding gave them their special rhythms and character; and, very curiously, in North America it took cross-breeding with a second foreign culture to eventually produce jazz—it was the music and dance of the slaves from Africa, mingled with old European jigs and lilts, that produced America's own folk art.

From the start, it was men who excelled in jazz dancing, but there are always exceptions, and one of the most important American dancers to conquer Europe between the two World Wars was a female exponent, the beautiful Josephine Baker, who reigned as queen of the Folies-Bergère in Paris for many years. Like her famous compatriot, Isadora Duncan, she was an artist of the highest integrity in her own field.

Josephine Baker was long-legged, lissom, and the most enticing shade of café-au-lait, which made her appear exquisitely dressed even when she was as near to stark naked as is compatible with art and beauty. Her costumes might have been ninety-seven per cent feather headdress, but the effect was not tinged with vulgarity; she made an art form out of cabaret in the would-be naughty world of Parisian night life—in other words, she had a supreme sense of style. And her personality was as warm and endearing as the colour of her skin. Again like Isadora Duncan, in life if not on the stage, Josephine Baker was a mother goddess who in her later years adopted a family of twelve children coloured everything but blue so that all the races could grow up together in love and harmony.

Isadora Duncan and Josephine Baker were two very unusual American women who brought fresh winds of change from the New World to the Old. In the early 1920's, Isadora was warmly accepted in Soviet Russia and was invited to found a school based on her ideals of a new free dance, which complemented the aspirations of a young revolutionary state. Although the school failed, her own very fluid and expressive arm movements had already made an impression on the style of classical ballet and they are gloriously visible in Soviet dancing; but jazz was not taken seriously as art in those serious times. Soviet ballet evolved on its own course almost totally cut off from the attitudes of mind of the early jazz era, and from the flippancy of the inter-war period, when the West thought only of a world without war while Russia was embarked on a completely new way of life.

JOSEPHINE BAKER

It was thirty years before Soviet and Western ballet were to meet each other, and in that time jazz rhythm and movement had subtly infiltrated all Western theatre dance. We grow up with jazz all around us, we are scarcely conscious of its influence, but it is reflected everywhere in our music, painting, and dance. It belongs to the twentieth century. To this day, Russia has never really been able to catch up with the true spirit and flavour of jazz. I believe this is the important difference, and it explains why some aspects of Soviet choreography have an oddly old-fashioned look for Western viewers. Apparently, one of the hazards—and ironies—of revolution, as opposed to evolution, is that the arts can become sadly detached from the mainstream of world influences while serving new ideologies.

However, that is not to underestimate Soviet ballet, which followed a fascinating course after the Revolution in 1917. Initially it faced three major problems. The first and greatest was that extremists wanted everything pertaining to the old Imperial way of life destroyed. Fortunately, wiser minds prevailed with the theory that the arts should be preserved and given to the people—so the ballet and its schools were saved.

Next was the problem that the general public was not educated to the arts, because they had been available to only a tiny minority before the Revolution. So concert parties of music and dance were sent to all the republics "to enlighten the masses"—as often as not, in vast makeshift halls. Obviously, the most spectacular items made the greatest impression in those surroundings and on the largely uninitiated audiences. They were given gingered-up highlights from classical ballets and acrobatic-style new choreographies: the ballerina held aloft on one hand ("adagio" dancing of this kind was fashionable in cabaret and music halls in the West at the same period).

Meanwhile, the system of training in Russia was undergoing some modernization after the choreographer Michael Fokine, earlier in the century, had introduced a natural expressiveness into ballet. It was the great teacher Agrippina Vaganova who formulated Soviet developments in training. Without altering the basic classical schooling, she greatly extended the range of movement and elevation. She had to evaluate the aesthetics of the new acrobatic choreography, which she welcomed insofar as it gave more pliancy to the dancers' bodies, but she had reservations: "Choreographically, eccentric-acrobatic elements should occupy only the modest one percent that they are worth."

The final problem was to find a formula for new ballets that would be both politically appropriate to the Revolution and theatrically successful with the mass public. At first, choreographers felt obliged to invent an original system that discarded classical rules;

however that approach bred dancers without technique, so it could not last, and *The Sleeping Beauty* was re-staged in 1922 but with adaptations—especially of the mimed scenes telling the story in gestures, because, although understood by the old upper-class public, the set language of gesture was incomprehensible to newcomers. These scenes were replaced by dance. But the classical ballets were essentially fantasy products of the old regime. A brief attempt at genuine avant-garde, which should have been well suited to a new social order, was unacceptable to the unsophisticated audience, while over-realistic subjects like hydroelectric power-station workers could not compete with the obstinately popular classics.

After ten years—not very long considering the extent of social upheaval—the voice of the Revolution found itself. *The Red Poppy*, produced in Moscow in 1927, was the first of the "liberation of oppressed peoples" genre—the Soviet heroic ballet—of which *The Flames of Paris* and *Spartacus* have been the other most successful examples. By this time the public was beginning to be readier for subtlety; thus the time was ripe in the 1930's for the lyrical-dramatic *The Fountain of Bakhchisarai* and Prokofiev's *Romeo and Juliet*, which, with its fine score, is the Soviet classic that has most influenced the West.

A diminishing problem during the formative years of Soviet ballet was the drain of top dancers and choreographers leaving the country from 1911 onwards—first, to join the Monte Carlo–based Diaghilev ballet, which stood for everything creatively interesting as opposed to Imperial ballet conservatism, and second, to escape the Revolution itself. The problem was effectively met by the two-hundred-year-old ballet schools and the network of new Soviet schools set up throughout the republics, thanks to which there was no shortage of legendary names; among them Marina Semyonova, who was purely classical; Olga Lepeshinskaya, of incredible technique and verve; Natalia Dudinskaya, warm and brilliant; and the ravishingly delicate, yet dramatic, Alla Shelest. Also the men—Konstantin Sergeyev, Alexei Yermolayev, the superb dancer and choreographer Vakhtang Chaboukiani, and many, many more. The name that reached the greatest international renown was that of Galina Ulanova.

Ulanova was born in St. Petersburg in 1910, the daughter of two dancers at the Imperial Maryinsky Theatre. What better start in life could there be for a ballerina? Since children are given to crossing their parents' wishes, Ulanova resisted the life destined for her. She did not want to enter the ballet school, she was unwilling to accept her fate, she would rather have been climbing trees and boating on the river with ordinary children of her age. The lurking desire to be free followed her through her student years, kept in check by her sense of duty, until full mastery allowed her to develop as an artist. Then the dance claimed and won her, not because she was interested in displaying her fine technique, but because she could use it to interpret the poetic heroines she understood so well. She needed some touch of tragedy in her roles. *The Sleeping Beauty*'s happy princess did not absorb her, she found the role "conventional." Her fulfillment came with *The Fountain of Bakhchisarai* and *Romeo and Juliet*. Their eternal heroines, caught in a love surpassing death, were perfect for her dance-acting through which she unfolded their tragic emotional conflicts with seamlessly beautiful grace. I have never seen another dancer with her liquid quality of movement, each step melting into the next with an inevitability that built its own tension. Ulanova symbolizes the triumph of Soviet ballet.

Another artist who has established her own inimitable style is Maya Plisetskaya, the opposite side of the coin to Ulanova. Plisetskaya's dancing is regal, dominating, sensual,

GALINA ULANOVA AND KONSTANTIN SERGEYEV IN *SWAN LAKE*

ULANOVA AND YURI ZHDANOV IN *ROMEO AND JULIET*

and magnificently powerful. Her movements are expansive, her elevation soaring, each limb stretches a little beyond the limits of possibility. She is the archetypal Soviet dancer.

Where Soviet and Western ballet training differ is in Russia's more acrobatic style and the West's more restrained development of pre-Revolutionary technique. Also in the ballets themselves. The West has exploited every aspect of one-act ballets, especially plotless interpretations of music in pure dance. The Soviet public might not initially have been receptive to these, but now I think they are eager for greater variety in modern choreography, and there is a serious effort being made in that direction. However, the differences between Soviet ballet and that of the West are still extreme: consider on the one hand the bombastic *Ivan the Terrible* produced in Moscow in 1975, and on the other *Le Tombeau de Couperin*, a ballet of patterns without story, soloists, or emotion, given the same year by New York City Ballet.

However, creation and training are two separate functions. Creation is vulnerable to every prevailing influence, but training traditions are extremely durable, and this is where the Soviet ballet's greatest strength has remained. It is conversely just where much of the West, especially America and Britain, faced a long struggle. Without the Russian or French type of long-established schools, where generation after generation can follow illustrious predecessors, it was hard to develop an advanced technique and appropriate style. The technique must be worked day after day from an early age—very difficult to arrange without special schools—and the question of style added to the problem because the classical ballets are nineteenth-century conceptions of even earlier periods. How could an American youth, born into the age of blue jeans, suddenly adopt the manners of a medieval prince hunting swans with a crossbow? The British found it somewhat easier because their life is more old-fashioned and many of the old theatre traditions are still preserved. Also because during the thirties, Ninette de Valois produced *Giselle, Coppélia, The Nutcracker, Swan Lake,* and *The Sleeping Beauty* at Sadler's Wells as a deliberate policy to give British ballet a firm basis in the standard classics. She was in fact the only ballet director at that time to understand the importance of giving full-evening ballets in their entirety (elsewhere in the West only excerpts were seen). But British ballet then was only a small local product, it had no impact outside the country. The major influence in the Western world was a large group of expatriate Russians who come under the generic heading "Ballets Russes" (Ballet Russe de Monte Carlo, Ballet Russe de Colonel de Basil, Original Ballet Russe, et cetera, et cetera).

Ballets Russes was sometimes one group, sometimes another. They split and had lawsuits—one side won the choreography, the other side got the scenery and costumes—so neither could produce a complete ballet. It was a homeless, moving mass of excitement. There was never a moment without rumour, rows, and temperament in abundance, and the whole added up on the stage to something dynamic and glamourous. There has been nothing quite like it since. The dancers had powerful personalities; they threw themselves onto the stage ready to burn it up, and almost did. A lot of the dancing was indifferent by today's standards, but the stars were superb—never to be forgotten.

Alexandra Danilova, of the slender legs someone so aptly called "witty," was indescribably vivid. A total artist, whose least flick of a finger made its point, she never smudged an effect, every movement said exactly what she wanted it to say—and with what gaiety! If I think of a dancer winning over an entire audience with one provocative smile, I

MAYA PLISETSKAYA IN *ROMEO AND JULIET*

IRINA BARONOVA IN *LE COQ D'OR*   TCHERNICHEVA AND SHABELEVSKY IN *SCHÉHÉRAZADE*

SARATOGA WITH ALEXANDRA DANILOVA

TAMARA TOUMANOVA AND LÉONIDE MASSINE IN *LE TRICORNE*

MASSINE IN *GAÎTÉ PARISIENNE* AND *SARATOGA*

think of Danilova. Fanny Elssler, in 1840, must have won the American public in much the same way; her dancing, her acting, her sexy charm must have been very like Danilova's. In retirement too, one can see that Danilova loses none of her fascination as she teaches young dancers and gives them some of her own magic. She came from the Leningrad ballet school shortly after the Revolution and is one of the many displaced Russian dancers who have settled in America. Some carry an air of Chekhovian nostalgia, some are buoyant and bubbling like Danilova.

What a contrast was the dark beauty of Tamara Toumanova, "The Black Pearl of Ballets Russes," a face to stare at and envy, with her large eyes, long lashes, beautiful brow, and chiselled nose! Toumanova came on the stage with an aura of mysterious tragedy, she was like the Byzantine empress Theodora—but born in the Far East on a train near Shanghai! Irina Baronova had something of Toumanova's imposing power and some of Danilova's wit and humour, yet she was not remotely like either. She expressed everything with

MASSINE IN *ST. FRANCIS*

the sheer assurance of her dancing, but no one could be more perceptive in her acting, especially in light comedy. She was the most versatile of all. For dramatic ability there was Lubov Tchernicheva, no longer a ballerina but a powerful actress. There were marvellous men too—Leon Woizikovsky, David Lichine, André Eglevsky, and the incomparable Igor Youskevitch. And dominating the picture was Léonide Massine.

As a very young man, Massine had left Moscow to join Serge Diaghilev's Ballets Russes—the original of that name—in Paris. He was so attractive, with very black eyes and such an irresistible, slightly withdrawn manner, that everyone who saw him must have been overcome. He was no less attractive in his eighties, especially when he happened to give one of his rare smiles or a laugh. In 1914 Diaghilev needed a new choreographer; he had an unerring instinct for hidden talents and gave the twenty-year-old dancer an opportunity to create ballets under his shrewd guidance. Massine justified the risk and proved one of the most individual of the great choreographers. He had an unusual use of movements and steps—always going in an unexpected direction—which he manipulated to ingenious effect in comedy ballets full of detailed characterization and infectious gaiety. There are his serious works, too, including the symphonic ballets—to Tchaikovsky's Fifth, Brahms' Fourth, Beethoven's Seventh, and Berlioz's *Symphonie Fantastique.* They are not danced now, and more's the pity, but *Le Beau Danube, Le Tricorne,* and *Boutique Fantasque* are among the ever-brilliant ballets of his enormous output. Massine was no mean dancer either, and his precision and magnetism are unforgettable.

The Ballets Russes, in all its various combinations with its many artists, blazed through London every summer, until the war years, when it toured the length and breadth of the United States in indescribable discomfort, sitting up for long train journeys because its managements were too stingy to pay for sleepers—indeed, the dancers were lucky if they got their salaries! Cramped legs clambered out of train compartments, through stage doors, and onto stages—a different one each night for months on end—yet they did not let their public down. They brought a vision of dance as a thrilling spectacle of beauty, colour, and giant-sized personalities encased in the magical make-up and clothing of another species. How could they not sow ambition in young hearts? American ballet came to life in the aura of the Ballets Russes, whose great influence was in the many types of ballet represented in the repertoire. American Ballet Theatre is the company that at this time most nearly carries its inheritance.

In their enthusiasm for the Ballet Russe, American audiences began to accept that men *could* do ballet, but only Russian men. At least that was the prejudice, and it was not easy to remove. The fascinating thing is to follow the quite unorthodox route by which the change was ultimately accomplished—through the American musicals and movies that had reached such a height of perfection in the hands (and feet) of Fred Astaire.

By the mid 1930's, various choreographers were beginning to make ballets with typically American themes: Massine's *Union Pacific,* Eugene Loring's *Yankee Clipper,* George Balanchine's *Alma Mater*—as well as his *Slaughter on Tenth Avenue,* a ballet choreographed for the Broadway musical *On Your Toes.* Loring made a ballet on Billy the Kid in 1938. Agnes de Mille created *Rodeo* in 1942, and Jerome Robbins triumphed with *Fancy Free* in 1944. Here at last were cowboys, folk heroes, sailors, and contemporary men. They cut through the previously rarefied atmosphere of ballet and gave it a modern crew-cut image. John Kriza personified this new type, and native Americans were at last established in what had once been the domain of the Russian-born. But there was still one

AGNES DE MILLE'S *RODEO* WITH RICHARD BEATTY, JOHN KRIZA, AND LEO DUGGAN

JEROME ROBBINS' *FANCY FREE* WITH ROBBINS, KRIZA, HAROLD LANG, JANET REED, AND MURIEL BENTLEY

ERIK BRUHN IN *PRINCESS AURORA*, 1949

more step to go to reach a fully classical style that was free of old mannerisms—a style as clean as the lines of modern architecture.

The dancer who revealed this perfect image of a twentieth-century classical dancer came from the oldest still extant school of all, the school of August Bournonville in Copenhagen. Erik Bruhn was trained entirely in this system, which had continued unchanged from the time of Bournonville's death in 1879. Yet nothing could be more pure and modern. It was because Bournonville had brought great respect to the ballet profession that Copenhagen was never without first-rate male dancers, even when they were as rare as golden eagles elsewhere; and in the 1950's Erik Bruhn, a golden eagle if ever there was one, set the style for classical dancing in our time. With his perfect amalgam of virtuosity and elegance, his beautiful line and handsome appearance, he gave inspiration to all the generations growing up after World War II, which he had spent as a student in the Royal Theatre school, appearing frequently with the other children in the company performances as is the charming custom in Bournonville's repertoire.

Soon after the War, London became the dance centre of the world, with a public avid for every national and international company. The effervescent French were led by Roland Petit with his brilliantly original choreography—each ballet a surprise and a delight. Petit, a star himself, but a generous one, loves to create and enhance other stars around him. For the magnetic personality of Jean Babilée, he made *Le Jeune Homme et la Mort*, with Nathalie Philippart as The Woman. They made a violent counterpart to Nijinsky and Karsavina in *Le Spectre de la Rose*. For himself and Zizi Jeanmaire, Petit created a fiery and sensuous Carmen that was markedly more powerful than the nineteenth-century ballet pastiches flavoured with Spain like vanilla in a cake.

The real Spanish dancing is different again, and curiously self-contained. It is rich in rhythm and refined technique, but being essentially folk dance it doesn't transfer easily to the professional stage. It needed the beauty, the warm personality, the *artistry* of La Argentina, who died very young, in 1936, to interpret the great variety of regional dances in sophisticated theatrical form—but then, she was one of the world's great artists, as was her contemporary, Vicente Escudero. Both of them were full-blooded stars.

Escudero was absolute master of the part-Moorish, part-gypsy flamenco, which is both music and dance. It belongs to Andalusia, where it inhabits the gypsy caves and small cafés. Flamenco is a matter of inspired improvisation within strict rhythmic rules, and in the close proximity of café-concert, where the dancers' ruffled skirts brush the tables at every twist and turn, the enthusiasts who are crowded around the dance floor follow each nuance with informed appreciation. For gypsies it is a different matter altogether to reproduce that art night after night at a precise hour in the commercial theatre. Only performers who can adopt theatre discipline without forfeiting spontaneity succeed as international stars. Escudero blazed a trail that was taken up by Antonio, an electrifying dancer of flamenco and particularly of the language of foot and heel beats called zapateado. He has such control that he can make his zapateado sound like fine rain pattering on the stage.

Antonio and his partner Rosario started the post-war cult of Spanish dance. During the last thirty years many others have pounded the stages of the world with their feet to the accompanying clatter of castanets; but the greatest of them all was a compact powerhouse of energy and controlled abandon named Carmen Amaya, who, like Antonio, had the discipline to conform to the laws of theatre, repeating the same movements with fresh spontaneity for seven performances a week.

Amaya was born in 1913 among the gypsies of Barcelona who dance before they can speak. Rhythm and music are the air they breathe from earliest infancy, and a few notes of the guitar are sufficient for arms to start circling the air in typical Spanish patterns as fingers snapped their accents. Amaya was a dancer to the marrow of her bones and a prisoner of her own genius to the end of her life. From the age of eight, when she first danced in Paris, she was breadwinner for relations who clung to her in numbers that increased in ratio to her fame, so that her tours resembled a gypsy camp always on the move. Some like to suggest that Carmen Amaya could scarcely write, but, working incessantly at rehearsal and performance, what time or need did she have for other means of expression? What mattered far more was her intuition. She was instinctively receptive and acquisitive, like a jackdaw, of everything that could feed her artistic fire. Yet with so much passion pouring out on the stage, she remained unsophisticated as a woman. Her life was simple, without scandal and with few rewards—the absolute reverse of the most famous "Spanish" dancer of the nineteenth century, Lola Montez, who was not Spanish at all but Irish, and very much more knowledgeable about men than about dance.

Lola's real name was Marie Gilbert and she was exceedingly beautiful in face and figure, with bronze skin and forget-me-not blue eyes. No one knew better how to charm the birds off the trees when she wanted to be ladylike. On other occasions she could perform her scandalous dance with spiders made of whalebone and rubber, or appear in scanty costumes, or attack a corps-de-ballet dancer with a dagger or the editor of an unfavourable review with a horsewhip. Lola Montez was quite a girl; when in 1846 she

LOLA MONTEZ

LA ARGENTINA

VICENTE ESCUDERO

ANTONIO

CARMEN AMAYA

A SPANISH CAFÉ, PRE-WORLD WAR I

wanted to dance in Munich she contrived to enter unannounced into the presence of Ludwig I of Bavaria and expose her beautiful naked bosom before his startled face. The King capitulated at once, allowing her to rule his life, and his kingdom, for a couple of years and honouring her with several titles. She must have been among the most successful combinations of beauty and sheer gall in the history of dance—if one could call it dance. Suddenly she decided to make amends by dedicating the rest of her life, which was to be much shorter than she could have guessed, extremely, to helping fallen women, and in that worthy occupation she died in 1861, aged forty-three, in New York, where she is buried.

Carmen Amaya too died young, at barely fifty, but she had literally danced herself to death. A spare, sinewy figure in man's costume, she could defy the rhythmic laws of flamenco without ever overstepping them, dancing counter-time and counter-counter-time with unerring precision. She was the only woman who could equal a man in flamenco, the most masculine of dances. This virility of men's flamenco made a strong impression on the public at a crucial time for ballet in the late 1940's and 1950's.

RUDOLF NUREYEV IN *VIVACE*

Within that period of a few short years it seemed that ballet became suddenly English, French, Danish, and American, and young men everywhere were dancing athletically, enthusiastically, and, most important of all, successfully. Two outstanding dancers, Jacques d'Amboise and Edward Villella, really caught the American public. Men who had been reluctantly persuaded to watch ballet were heard saying as they left the theatre, "Those dancers must be incredibly fit—they're like athletes." Respect crept into their voices.

And so the mid-century came and went. In the ballet world the ballerinas had taken the limelight for far too long: now the men were returning in strength to claim their share. And they were fortified, from 1956 on, by the excitement surrounding Soviet companies seen for the first time since the Revolution.

It was when ballet in the West had just settled down to comfortable activity and satisfying recognition that Rudolf Nureyev arrived, supersonically it seemed, from Russia, and nothing in dance was ever quite the same as it had been before. The temperature rose. The age of women's lib became in dance the age of men's lib, and the age of superpowers became also the age of superstars. Thus came to an end one hundred years that could be summed up in a caricature of 1860 captioned, "The disagreeable thing about ballerinas is that they sometimes bring along a male dancer with them."

Nureyev, the Tartar born on a long train journey across Siberia to Vladivostok, on the Sea of Japan, and raised in Ufa, at the foot of the Ural Mountains, graduated from the Leningrad ballet school in 1958 to make his début straight into principal roles at the Kirov Theatre. To explain his charisma would be as impossible as explaining any other great star. He is the exact opposite of Fred Astaire in that he knew from the moment he first saw dance, at the age of six, that that was what he must do; but no one helped him, and he was seventeen by the time he reached Leningrad. Astaire spent years in the profession before achieving fame, but Nureyev went straight from school to the top. Astaire's charisma is relaxed, Nureyev's is tense. They are both geniuses, yet Astaire is at ease in retirement whereas Nureyev will guard his passion until his last breath.

Nureyev has an impeccable lineage in classical training that reaches back in a direct line to the great teachers of France and Italy in the early 1800's. Nureyev's teacher was Alexander Pushkin, a charming little man with few words but a prodigious understanding of the body's ability to master movement. Although all ballet classes follow a basic structure of exercises progressing to short dance sequences, there are a thousand and one ways in which those little segments of movement can be ordered and combined. The teacher

LA SYLPHIDE   *THE SLEEPING BEAUTY*

ordains each day the number of repetitions of each exercise, and in which directions and combinations they shall be done. The secret of a good teacher is in knowing just how to build the succession of exercises for each day's work. Some steps should be slow, others fast; the limbs must be prepared in the right time to cope with them. All these things Pushkin understood perfectly, so that an intelligent brain, following exactly what he set, would know just which muscles came into use for each movement, and the precise coordination of limbs necessary to achieve the required result.

Pushkin taught for many years at the Kirov School in Leningrad. Among *his* teachers had been Nicholas Legat, whom he somewhat resembled in face and stature as well as in temperament. Legat was a famous dancer who left Russia as an émigré from the Revolution and settled in 1926 in London, where he lived and gave classes in a building next to the present Royal Ballet School. At the age of twelve, I took lessons with him for a short time. He was enchanting in his benevolent good humour and occasional elfin fancy. Like all Russian professors, he could be quite sarcastic by way of reproof, but it was always a

MOMENT   AUREOLE

kindly sarcasm. I never saw him lose his temper as some of his colleagues did. He conducted his class from the piano, on which he accompanied the exercises himself, adding amusing little trills and flourishes from time to time. Sometimes he got up to clarify a step, but mostly the pupils knew what was required from his instructions given with the dancer's customary hand semaphore. The pattern his class followed was known by all who had studied with him a short while. In fact, a ballet class is similar to a crossword puzzle in that once one knows the teacher's formula, it is quite easy to pick up the steps—doing them is another matter altogether!

Legat had been a pupil in St. Petersburg of the great teacher Christian Johansson, a Swede who had trained in Copenhagen with Bournonville, who had studied in Paris with Auguste Vestris in 1820. Johansson used to accompany his lessons on a little violin, as did all the early dancing masters, and he purposely made patches on the floor with water when he wanted to teach his pupils to keep their balance under any circumstances; all the old teachers had fiendish tricks like that, but their combined store of knowledge, treasured in the Leningrad ballet school, is every dancer's heritage.

Nureyev has both a passion for this classical schooling of his upbringing and an insatiable need to explore for himself every new frontier of movement. When he came to the West in 1961, driven by the compulsion for new choreographic experience, he was twenty-three and not only astounding in virtuosity but with an inexplicable onstage magnetism that made people talk of Nijinsky for lack of any other comparison. He is, however, not a second Nijinsky but the first Nureyev.

He soon set about the classical ballets, determined to make the principal male role at least as important as the ballerina's. This came as something of a jolt to those of us accustomed to having most of the limelight, and it was harder still on our partners, who had spent so many years respectfully dedicated to "showing off" their ballerinas, but there was logic in it. Nureyev reasoned that "pas de deux" means a *dance* for two, not one partner dancing and the other walking about. Like all pioneers, he had to force the issue some-

THE MALE SUPPORTED BY HIS BALLERINA

WITH FONTEYN IN ROLAND PETIT'S *PARADISE LOST* AND DIANE GRAY IN MARTHA GRAHAM'S *NIGHT JOURNEY*

what, and his tactic was criticized as pure egoism, nothing more. As a natural conservative, it was a little while before I appreciated the revolution taking place around me, but I respected his intelligence and acknowledged the wisdom of turning oneself into a movable object when faced with irresistible force—although I didn't give in without a struggle. But anyone who generates so much sheer excitement onstage as Nureyev makes the stuff of magic, and that is what matters. Time and time again I have seen, and have been in, performances when all the members of the company excelled themselves because of the tiger pacing in the wings, practising his steps till the last second, changing his shoes six times to find the best ones (like a tennis champion with his racquets) and cursing them in foul language for being too old, too still, too tight, or too loose, or just for existing to annoy him. As he makes his entrance, all eyes are rivetted on the tiger walking with such dignity and grace to centre stage, looking very concentrated within himself. He makes the preparation for his "variation," or solo, with utmost care and accuracy, and leaps into the air as though pouncing at a prey three times his size. The variation lasts one minute or one minute and a

NUREYEV AND FONTEYN BACKSTAGE

LE CORSAIRE

half, the tiger seems to fly above the heads of the corps de ballet, he finishes with a final thrust and holds his pose with an air of victory over dark forces that might have killed him. His breathtaking steps have looked sometimes as easy as a bird flying, sometimes dangerously impossible. The audience has lived through the experience with him.

That is the excitement and magic of Nureyev, and it brought new life to the old ballets just when they were in danger of losing the younger public. Unquestionably, the idea of a dancer with the attraction of a pop singer brought teen-agers to the ballet in droves and, by his example, dancers still in training raised their sights at the prospect of a world in which they might become superstars too. The standard of virtuosity rose, literally, by leaps and bounds.

For Nureyev it was only the first phase. He went on to work with the contemporary choreographers in ballet and modern dance movement, and right into the Martha Graham technique, which is so totally different in origin and principle from classical ballet. It was a giant leap from Leningrad to Martha Graham, and it made him symbolic of the super-modern ballet dancer who is master of the past and present and is ready for the future. Nureyev strikes out beyond the current scene, leading the way. Even today no other dancer fills a London or New York theatre for three weeks on one name alone as *Nureyev and Friends* or just *Nureyev* does each year. This is what I mean when I say that the era of the ballerina is over.

I don't want to suggest that there are no more ballerinas. On the contrary, they dance far better than ever before, their technique is breathtaking, they perform miracles, but they no longer rule the roost—or whatever the equivalent is for swans. In the 1930's it was somehow taken for granted that the ballerina was the apex of any performance, whether or not it was strictly true—and sometimes it was not. Nevertheless, ballerinas were always given the best dressing rooms, all the bouquets, and reams of adulation. There was a clearly defined conception of how they should look and what they should dance. They wore tutu ballet skirts more often than not, and were judged on their interpretations of *Giselle, Les Sylphides, Swan Lake,* and *The Nutcracker*—or excerpts therefrom. In photographs they were usually serious and soulful; off-stage they were well-groomed.

The conception now is more diffused. Ballerinas are no longer judged solely on their classical repertoire—the fantastic Suzanne Farrell of the New York City Ballet hardly ever dances those roles, but she is a top-flight ballerina. Onstage they still sometimes wear ballet skirts, although more likely they will appear in all-over tights (leotards) that enhance

PETROUCHKA

DON QUIXOTE

PUSH COMES TO SHOVE

LE SPECTRE DE LA ROSE

THEME AND VARIATIONS

NATALIA MAKAROVA IN *SWAN LAKE*

none but the faultless, bulgeless figure which, luckily, they all have. In ordinary life they can often be found disguised in blue jeans and T-shirts.

Meanwhile, men look their best and most masculine in leotards, and that is how they are seen in ninety per cent of new ballets. The top stars are judged now, as ballerinas were before, on certain classical works—mainly *Giselle, Le Corsaire, Don Quixote,* and *Swan Lake,* or pas de deux therefrom—and in life they dress in the latest elegant couture, or trendy, casual fashions. They often occupy the best dressing rooms and receive bouquets. The honours now are fairly evenly divided, or weighted a little in favour of the men, which is as it was in the beginning.

If one is going to single out names from all the magnificent, beautiful creatures now roaming the stages of the world, Mikhail Baryshnikov and Natalia Makarova are two who, like Nureyev, have their roots in Leningrad and have bloomed in the West. It does seem to be an arrangement that breeds an especially fine strain of artist.

Baryshnikov is a miracle of weightlessness who does the impossible with the nonchalance of a Fred Astaire. He goes from extraordinary classical virtuosity to modern ballets as easily as a chameleon changes colour, and he expresses the sheer joy of dancing. Yet his dancing is shaded by a haunting, mysterious melancholy that seems to lie behind the joy, setting him apart like a lone poet who sees beyond the vision of other men. One cannot tell if he sees beyond dance to a way of life that would bring him greater fulfillment, or whether he seeks to ward off the bitter-sweet flavour of complete achievement. What is certain is that he is physically a dancer of astounding ability, and artistically one who wears his roles like a glove, not dominating them but enclosing himself in them.

Natalia Makarova, supreme ballerina, evokes another touch of mystery. Her body and limbs have the strength and flexibility of the finest steel, she is absolutely sure and authoritative on the stage, yet with it all she combines the vulnerability of a little waif or a helpless leaf in the autumn wind. This fascinating balance between power and frailty gives her dancing a quality that is hers alone. Each ballerina must have her own distinction, she must take what others have done before and make it her own. This Makarova does with the classics she was trained on, yet she also has conquered contemporary works for which her training did not totally prepare her. She is now at the height of her powers.

These are but two of the great dancers in whose care dance is truly fulfilling its magical purpose. That purpose was quite out of step when I first joined in the dance. Now, thanks to artists like Astaire, the Danes, the French, the British, the Americans, and the Russians—and the Spaniards too—we can hope and expect it will never falter again.

DANCE EXPERIMENTAL

People called her a great artist—a Greek goddess—
but she was nothing of the kind.
She was something quite different from anyone or anything else.

—GORDON CRAIG

Isadora Duncan is more difficult to describe, explain, categorize, or summarize than any other dancer, even the mysterious Nijinsky. She does not fit into any category because she was a poet of motion. A poet uses the words we all know and, following his own inspiration, creates a language personal only to him. That is what Isadora did with human movement. In a way, ridiculous as it sounds, she was not interested in what goes by the name of "dancing." Dancing has rules. It has steps, movements of the legs, hopping, changing weight; even the most primitive dances are composed of certain repetitions which, no matter how simple, constitute steps. When it comes to folk dancing, the steps begin to exist for their own sake, but Isadora had not the least interest in such distinctions, and the most highly developed technique of all, that of ballet, she abhorred.

We make the mistake of thinking of her in terms of theatre because dance now is exclusively a matter of entertainment. Whether presented on a stage or enjoyed spontaneously in a nightclub, it belongs to our leisure hours, certainly not to our religious life or material survival. Isadora tried to return dance to its original spiritual purpose, but to disseminate it through the then available channels. I doubt that she was ever fully aware of this conflict. She would dance as readily in a salon or garden as on a stage; the location was of minor importance because she was not a theatre artist except in the sense that temples or churches in early history were the "theatres" of community life. But that was long before the modern stage, framed in its proscenium arch, created its own rules for making a genuine truth out of artificiality by means of technique and art.

In the modern sense of theatre Isadora was an amateur. She saw nothing incongruous in explaining with words what she had tried to express in her dance if she thought the audience had not grasped her message. It did not bother her that theatre convention expects the performance to stand or fall on its own merit, and explanations to be confined to the program notes—she was on a different track altogether. Her theatre should have been a temple, as she sought the "divine expression of the human spirit" and what she called "the truth of my being."

This truth was compounded more of emotion than anything else; instinct was her guide, while logic and reason were but passing visitors. She wanted to become nature itself, to be the sky, the waves, the breeze, not to transmute them by any known formula of art. So she had to invent her own formula. She had to find how she herself would run or skip if joy motivated that reaction, how she herself would bow down if sorrow crushed her; then she used those movements and gestures as her dance steps.

Such people as Isadora—one of a kind—seem to appear in the world without rhyme or reason. It is possible that we are aware of them only when their appearance coincides with a period that is ready for them, as was her case. It is possible that twenty years earlier or later no one would have been interested in her message—or perhaps she herself would have communicated it in a different way; who can tell? In any event, she was born at the right time, in 1878, and California was probably the best place for her to grow up because both the climate and the intellectual atmosphere induced a certain freedom of movement and thought.

AT THE PARTHENON

Isadora's father deserted the family early on, and her mother struggled to support the four children, two sons and two daughters, by teaching music. Of the four, Isadora was the one who gained most from the combination of a Scottish father and Irish mother; she had beauty of face and form, inherent musicality, a generous heart, and all the compelling charm of the Irish that makes others follow wherever they lead. As a child she had no hesitation in teaching her younger playmates to dance, regardless of the fact that she knew next to nothing about it herself. Later on it was only natural that the whole family would be swept off to Chicago, New York, and Europe in pursuit of Isadora's compulsion to dance in her own way. She believed that Hellenic Greece held the key to that secret of movement she desired, so, as soon as her initial impact on Europe had brought in a small nest egg of money, the Duncan family continued via Venice, and thence, following ecstatically but in considerable discomfort the route of Ulysses, to Athens. It was 1903. Isadora had reached the age of twenty-five without encountering love. She did not need it—her vitality and emotions were entirely absorbed in her quest.

Their first Athenian dawn found all five Duncans ascending the Acropolis and be-

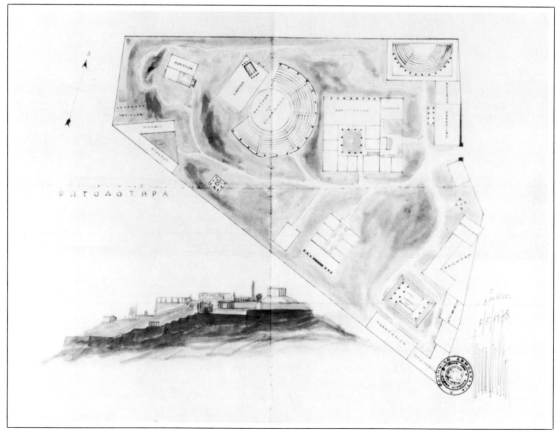

GROUND PLAN OF THE DUNCAN COMMUNE IN ATHENS

holding with mystical reverence the overwhelming and lofty perfection of the Parthenon. They had, in Isadora's words, "gained that secret middle place from which radiates in vast circles all knowledge and beauty." Now her task was to capture that beauty.

> *For the last four months each day I have stood before this miracle of perfection wrought of human hands . . . and I did not dare move, for I realized that of all the movements my body had made none was worthy to be made before a Doric Temple. And as I stood thus I realized that I must find a dance whose effect was to be worthy of this Temple—or never dance again. . . . For many days no movement came to me. And then one day came the thought: These columns which seem so straight and still are not really straight, each one is curving gently from the base to the height, each one is in flowing movement, never resting, and the movement of each is in harmony with the others. And as I thought this my arms rose slowly towards the Temple and I leaned forward—and then I knew I had found my dance, and it was a Prayer.*

Out of such immature ecstasy Isadora created her dance; it cannot be repeated or imitated or taught, for, of all her pupils, only those she kept with her and inspired herself learned anything—and then, human as she was above all else, when they grew up to be successful on their own account and show some independence, she was not too pleased!

In their first euphoric days on the Acropolis the Duncan family, as of one mind, had decided to honour the ancient Greeks by building an arts commune where they would live the homespun life, with their heads in lofty thought and their feet in sandals. They threw themselves into this extraordinary and hopeless project with typical fervour, scouring the region until they came upon a hill at Kopanos, declared by Isadora's brother Raymond, as he cast his staff to the ground, to be the chosen site. Raymond drew up ambitious plans to include a house, a small temple, a Greek theatre, a library, and various outbuildings; sheep were to graze on the slopes. Isadora bought the hill at considerable expense and likewise the special stone, transported by donkey, to construct substantial walls for the house, which was modelled on Agamemnon's ancient palace at Mycenae—nothing less.

The house was completed—it is now being restored as a Duncan museum—but the rest of the scheme was doomed from the start. For one thing, it became far more costly than anticipated and, in any case, Isadora was to find out that she was the last person in the world for the truly simple life. When she discovered love and luxury, she took to them both fervently, often, near the end of her short life, spending her last penny on a bottle of the best champagne. Raymond was the true ascetic in the family; to the end of his days he wore robes, a beard, long hair, sandals—and, I suspect, a serious mien.

It gradually became clear that the Duncans' dream of re-living the artistic glories of ancient Greece could not materialize. Isadora's savings began to run low and the modern Athenians showed no enthusiasm for being swept back to their golden past by a family of eccentric Americans—the big hit of her performances was her Viennese waltz. Discouraged, she went alone at midnight to dance in the ruins of the Dionysus Theatre and then, ever restless—but secretly relieved?—she headed for Paris, Vienna, Budapest, Berlin, and Russia. She found romance, riches, fame, and tragedy.

She was nothing if not a bundle of contradictions. Without ever relinquishing her belief in the Greek dance of temple and arena, she also wanted to be a theatre star—she was happy to be applauded and acclaimed. She was eager to succeed as an artist, and indeed poets, musicians, painters, writers, sculptors, the theatre reformer Stanislavsky, and the designer Gordon Craig were devoted admirers—sometimes lovers. She bloomed in their company.

In her muddle-headed, instinctive Irish way she tried to do the impossible and a lot of the time she succeeded. I don't believe she fully understood what she was, or the true quality of her affinity with Greece. She was the mythological Mother Nature, the eternal woman. Her motivation, fixation, obsession was for children; through every crisis she clung to her dream of a school where a thousand children would live in joy and health in dance, and teach thousands more in ever-increasing numbers. She was not so much a liberated woman, in the rather narrow modern sense, as an all-embracing eternal earth mother. She was pure mother, not housewife. No one ever heard of Mother Nature having a husband, and no more could Isadora. In the end she married her wild Russian poet, Essenin, but not out of a sudden conversion to respectability; it was only because she saw in his curly golden head an image of her dead son as he would have grown up, and she could refuse him nothing, least of all the possibility of a passport to leave Russia with her.

The bizarrely simple and avoidable accident that had drowned her two children, trapped in a car as it slipped into the Seine during a violent storm, was a catastrophic tragedy. It tore her soul, left her not a second without pain and sorrow, and destroyed her life. Neither dance, nor champagne, nor lovers gave her peace ever more, until one day a long scarf, thrown unthinkingly around her neck, caught in the wheel of her car—driven by a young man she had instinctively recognized as a messenger of the gods—and took her swiftly to that place where her innocent children awaited her.

IN ''LA MARSEILLAISE''

WITH HER CHILDREN, DEIRDRE AND PATRICK   WITH HER STUDENTS AT GRUNEWALD, 1905

WITH HER STUDENTS, 1909

The measure of our inability to recognize basic truths of nature when we see them is that almost everything about Isadora's turbulent life that seemed natural and logical to her was sensational or scandalous to the civilized world.

Had Isadora as a young girl been able to see Anna Pavlova in her prime she would have understood that the technique of a highly trained ballet dancer is no more than absolute control of movement, the means by which the soul can be released and the spirit shine forth. But Isadora was a year or two older, and by the time she did see Pavlova she was so engrossed in carrying the torch of natural dance that she could not equate herself in any way with ballet. Yet I think it undeniable that in her free use of arm movements, Isadora influenced the ballet quite strongly. Oddly enough I cannot really see that she was the "Mother of Modern Dance," as she is often called, except that by taking dance back to the beginning she made it easier for others to start out again in new directions. To have some understanding of how and why she was able, with little more than emotion and personality, to make such a deep impression on artists and intellectuals, one must look at the state of dance during the last twenty years of the nineteenth century—which roughly coincided with the first twenty of Isadora's life.

In 1878, when Isadora was born, most of the capitals of Europe maintained state-supported opera houses whose ballet companies and schools provided at least a centre of training, whether it was put to serious artistic use or wasted on fripperies. In these areas ballet dancing retained varying degrees of quality and respect. Only London and New York lacked any backbone of subsidized professional ballet, and there the hapless student was at the mercy of individual teachers, of whom a handful knew their business and the rest taught "fancy dancing"—in other words, a garbled mixture of anything they happened to have seen or done themselves. Under those circumstances the old classical ballet that had been so highly esteemed in the mid-nineteenth century, particularly by the London public, degenerated into meaningless gyrations by inexpert chorus girls in the music hall. Their over-developed calf muscles were revealed all too clearly by the rigid, many-layered ballet skirts which had been shortened over the years expressly to display clever technique. In the process all grace and feminine allure had vanished along with art and magic.

It was the short-lived skirt dance, first seen at the Drury Lane Theatre in the 1870's, that heralded the first revolt. Skirt dancing, with its long, softly swirling dresses, defied traditional ballet costume and, although the steps themselves were quite childish, it was utterly modern in its time and caused an extraordinary sensation. Many an eager society lady,

"LES POULES," FOLIES-BERGÈRE

MARIANNA PITTERI IN "STAR OF HOPE"

REGINA BADET, PREMIÈRE DANSEUSE, PARIS OPERA

CONCERT POSTER FOR THE GRAND COMIC OPERA CO.

hoping to make a hit at some charitable affair and confident that she was well able to cope with the simple steps and gentle turns, not to mention the easy manipulation of her skirts, was dismayed to find herself flat on the floor, irretrievably entangled in her dress. No doubt this was what killed the dance off.

Perhaps without Kate Vaughan it would never have caught on at all, but she was a particularly appealing dancer who had the luck to get some decent ballet training. She had a classically beautiful face with large dark eyes that showed a trace of melancholy; her style was reminiscent of Tanagra figurines and she inspired the Pre-Raphaelite painters and poets who worshipped her. She was to her generation in England what Marie Taglioni had been to Paris forty years before: the expression of a new direction in the arts and, in spite of an occasional high kick—referred to by a stuffy critic as "this unpleasant step"—Kate was the harbinger of a return to artistry in dance before Isadora Duncan was even born.

The next lone spirit to add some personal enchantment to the generally abject state of theatre dance was a spirited English girl named Lottie Collins, who took the cancan, added a zest of English innocence, combined it with a ta-ra-ra-boom-de-ay, and made an admittedly music-hall number into something in which, "wild and wilder as the refrain grows, half maddened as the dancer seems to become, no one can reasonably detect one trace of vulgarity or immodesty in a single movement." With this simple little item Lottie took England and America by storm.

People were indeed rather easily pleased. What pleased them most was grand spectacle, and this must have reached its zenith in 1881 with *Excelsior,* a masterpiece (in six parts and twelve scenes) produced at La Scala Theatre, Milan, by the choreographer Luigi

LETTY LIND'S SKIRT DANCE   KATE VAUGHAN   LOTTIE COLLINS

Manzotti. The plot was no less than the rise of civilization, represented by technology struggling against the dark forces of ignorance. A colossal cast of five hundred depicted the invention of the steamship and the iron bridge, the construction of the Suez Canal in Egypt and the Mont Cenis Tunnel through the Alps, and the discovery of electricity. It ended in an apotheosis of enlightenment and peace. Transferred to Paris, to a theatre built specially for extravaganzas, it ran for a whole year. Manzotti was in his element with this type of ballet. In another production he found a pretext for eighteen horses, two elephants, and an ox.

Excelsior, with its dedication to spectacle and virtuosity at the expense of human values, epitomized the virtues and failings of nineteenth-century Italian ballet which vanished like a puff of smoke when dance caught up with expressionist developments in art and music. But *Excelsior* was also very much a product of old traditions. The Italians had always been masters of spectacle; almost everything we associate with theatre originated in the palaces of Italian dukes, princes, and kings. The sophistication of their productions still amazes. Given that the performances were based on allegories carefully reflecting the political objectives of the occasion—usually some form of alliance by marriage—the person devising them needed to be somewhat of a politically oriented Cecil B. DeMille, and a poet as well. One such man was Count Filippo d'Aglié at the Court of Savoy in the seventeenth century. What imagination! What masterly control of the whole paraphernalia of spectacle! The most extravagant theatre producer one could name would look impoverished beside the talents of d'Aglié. He wrote the scenarios and the verses—in Latin, Italian, or French—for over forty ballets, played several instruments, composed his own scores, and was known throughout Europe for the brilliance of his choreography. As a councillor of state he was naturally well aware of the power game to which these sumptuous occasions were dedicated.

Immense halls were put into service for such performances. Early illustrations show how the disposition of spectators and performers in these palace halls passed through various rearrangements until the now familiar form of theatre auditorium was reached. The most interesting phase was when performers used the stage and also descended from it to a large arena-like space in front. The only remaining example of this arena-stage combination is in the fascinating Farnese Theatre in the ducal palace at Parma, which, although destroyed by bombs in World War II, has been restored to its exact original form.

The theatre occupies an enormous unwanted armory on the second floor, and it was constructed purely to score a point of social rivalry. The Duke of Parma wanted to impress

EXCELSIOR, 1881

LA LIBERAZIONE DI TIRENNO E D'ARNEA, 1616

Cosimo de' Medici of Florence, who planned to stop off on his way home from a pilgrimage in 1618. The work was rushed through, never ceasing day or night, and a magnificent performance rehearsed, but Cosimo felt too exhausted by his journey and decided to take a shorter route home by boat. Everything was cancelled. Ten years went by before the theatre saw its first performance, and it must have been well worth the wait. Appropriately enough, a marriage uniting the Medici and Farnese houses provided the excuse for the superb spectacle, which included a ballet, an opera, a horse ballet led by the bridegroom, and a thrilling finale in which the arena was flooded to a depth of three feet for a battle of sea monsters while one hundred people descended from the ceiling on a cloud. The audience was in terror that the whole place would collapse under the weight of water, but all went off as planned. The son of the marriage, conceived perhaps that selfsame night, was so keen on dancing and theatre that he nearly bankrupted the entire state with his magnificent fêtes and celebrations.

IL FAVORE DEGLI DEI, 1690

COURT DANCE FROM TREATISE BY WILLIAM THE JEW

Dancing was no easy accomplishment for an enthusiastic amateur like this young duke. Even one hundred and fifty years before he was born, a dancing master called Domenico from the little town of Piacenza had summarized in detail the very exacting court dances: he listed twelve basic steps, and twenty-one different dances of his own composing. His pupil William the Jew, from Pesaro, worked thirty years to prepare a beautifully illustrated treatise bringing the subject up to date in 1463. Timing and "contra tempo" were among the niceties recommended for study.

Then there was Cesare Negri, nicknamed the Trombone—no one explains why—who was very demanding of his pupils. They had to turn out their feet like a modern ballet dancer, and master ten different kinds of pirouette. The Trombone was a much-travelled star dancer and choreographer in the exclusive world of courtiers. One can see that Italians were easily carried away by virtuosity, so it is understandable that Milan, already the centre of dance when Negri was born in 1536, should have become the centre of ballet technique at a later time. But excessive virtuosity always produces a reaction sooner or later.

One such came at the end of the eighteenth century. An important Italian choreographer, Salvatore Viganò, with his Spanish wife, Maria Medina, tried to bring a more naturalistic expressionism into ballet. They turned back to ancient Greece for their inspiration in subject, movement, and costume as Isadora was to do later. How similar they were can be judged from this description written by a lady in Vienna in 1793:

IL CARNEVALE LANGUENTE, TURIN, 1647

MARIA MEDINA VIGANÒ

Maria Medina wore nothing over her flesh-coloured tights but two or three crêpe skirts, one shorter than the other, gathered in at the waist by a dark-coloured belt. This belt was really all she wore, for the crêpe concealed nothing. As she danced her skirts rose and floated out, revealing her body, which in the natural-coloured tights appeared completely naked. The effect produced by this woman and the ballets her husband created for her was sensational; it was the triumphant culmination of an old art and a new manner.

The Viganòs were simply in advance of an approaching trend. Fashion, like virtuosity, reaches extremes which are followed by reaction, and the excesses of formal eighteenth-century brocade costumes, with their panniers and petticoats, were replaced by high-waisted, soft-flowing Empire styles vaguely inspired by Grecian robes. But then, in due course, weight and pomp gradually reconquered the scene.

THE VIGANÒS

Around 1900 the same pattern repeated itself after the excesses of whalebone corsetting, bustles, and bombazine. Kate Vaughan's fluttering, swirling skirts were a pointer towards liberation both off and on the stage, and the theatre was so wide open for anything new and attractive that a person who was scarcely a dancer at all was able to create an international sensation. She was Loie Fuller, a clever young lady from Illinois, who had started her career as an actress. Purely by chance she hit upon an original way to exploit the comparatively recent discovery of electricity. While in a play in London she had met a young officer of the Indian army who, on her return to New York, shipped over a sari of exquisitely fine material. It happened that she was draping the transparent cloud of silk around herself in front of a mirror and wondering how she could make it into a dress, when the sun's rays came through a window behind her and, shining through the stuff, made such a beautiful effect that she began to twist and float it around to watch the play of light.

This was enough to set her busy brain to work. With the help of her brothers she evolved a wide range of stage illusions, including illumination through glass in the floor, which had never been seen before. The Fire Dance, the Serpentine Dance, the Rainbow, and the Basket were among many numbers composed by swirling hundreds of yards of thistledown fabric in breathtaking movement and colour. The secret cut of these voluminous costumes was protected by her mother, who carried them in and out of the theatre closely wrapped.

Loie Fuller was as different from Isadora Duncan as theatre is from nature. Loie had theatrical sense in the highest degree: every detail of her staging, requiring a small army of electricians, was worked out and rehearsed in meticulous detail. She was, however, the first to admit that she was not much of a dancer. The only similarity between her and Isadora was summed up in Loie's words, talking about the ancient Greeks: "I believe that they studied more the impression that they wished to convey by their dancing than the actual way of dancing."

Loie's greatest successes were in Paris. On her first visit in 1892 she was dubious about appearing at the Folies-Bergère—the only management to accept her. However, she made such an impression there that she was quickly taken up by artists and intellectuals and especially the avant-garde group. A strong admiration for Marie Curie inspired her to create a Radium Dance. Her performances, however, were more gimmick than dance and did not endure. And as for Loie Fuller herself, she got very fat.

The only known precedent for Loie Fuller, one hundred years earlier, was the attractive Lady Hamilton, Lord Nelson's mistress, who was given to graceful amateur caperings

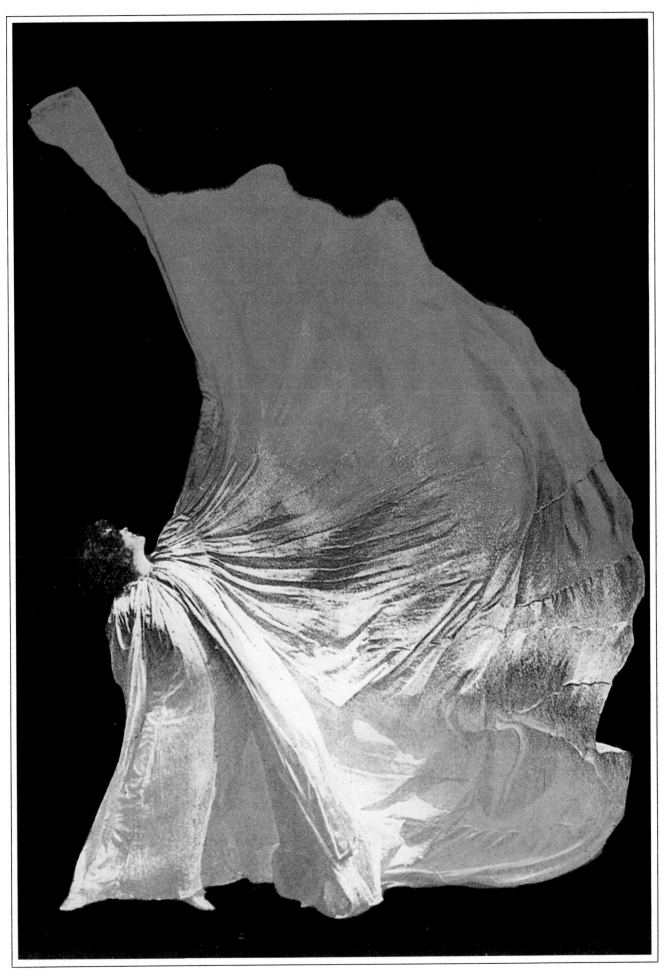

LOIE FULLER PERFORMING THE FIRE DANCE

at her salon in the British Embassy at Caserta. While doing one of her Viganò-type dances with a couple of floating scarves, it occurred to her to ask her acquiescent husband, the ambassador, to hold a candelabra behind her so that she danced in a luminous glow of gentle light.

What I find astonishing is that, following Loie Fuller's triumphs, no one combined her ideas with fully professional dancers in genuine choreographic invention until the 1950's, when Alwin Nikolais developed his "Sound and Vision Pieces." Nikolais manip-

THE SPIRAL   THE BASKET   THE SERPENTINE DANCE

ulates ideas, movements, colours, sounds, lights, and props like the magician he is, and the results are as startlingly as they are brilliantly theatrical.

The excitement caused by Loie Fuller and Isadora Duncan around 1900 made toe shoes and ballet skirts look decidedly old-fashioned. In Paris they persisted only at that bastion of classical ballet, the Opera, led from 1894 to 1940 by a splendid Milanese ballerina, Carlotta Zambelli. She danced until 1927, and then directed the school and ruled the ballet with benign severity. She was a dark-haired, sparkling-eyed woman of enormous energy, and she saved French-Italian training from certain decay in those days of doubtful artistic pretension when the likes of Regina Badet could claim to be "Danseuse de l'Opéra."

    In the midst of that curious conglomeration of virtuosity and bad taste at the turn of the century lived a delicate flower, a magical beauty, called Cléo de Mérode. Because the King of the Belgians was sensible enough to love her, Cléo is counted among the great courtesans of La Belle Époque, but obviously she was far too romantic to be of their kind (La Belle Otero, for example, was a stunning Spanish beauty and a personality, well able to fend for herself). Cléo de Mérode was sensitive and vulnerable. In Madrid she fell in love with a prince and he with her, wanting to marry her, although it was obviously an unrealizable ambition. His family, of course, forbade marriage to a dancer, and she returned sadly to the Paris Opera, where her fragility was somewhat out of place. When I look at her photographs I always imagine that I detect in her wistful eyes a rare artist unful-

CLÉO DE MÉRODE

filled. Unlike Carlotta Zambelli, she was not born in the right place at the right time. Carlotta was one of the "whalebone" ballerinas in the grand manner, strong and vivacious. In 1901 she was the last foreign guest ballerina invited to St. Petersburg.

By 1904 the young generation of St. Petersburg dancers, realizing that the pendulum swing towards technique had reached its limit and must now reverse, was hungry for the change. At first the new swing went wholly in the direction of truthful expression as revealed by a young choreographer, Michael Fokine. Fokine was dark, handsome, and a po-

CARLOTTA ZAMBELLI

etic revolutionary. He was able to call on two hundred years of ballet tradition—as well as the superb dancers it had produced—at the same time as he rejected its archaic aspects. He harked back to olden times; re-created romantic visions of the nineteenth century, of the exotic East, of old Russia, and classical Greece. But although his ballets were not modern or contemporary in subject, they were new in their approach to dance: for instance, he discarded pointe shoes almost completely, believing it ludicrous to see nymphs or supposed ladies of a harem dancing on their toes. It is amusing to reflect that Fokine, who is always placed so categorically with classical ballet, choreographed *The Firebird, Schéhérazade, Petrouchka*, and *Thamar* with scarcely a pure ballet step to be found in any of them, and only four of the dozens of female characters actually in toe shoes. It was, however, the age for discarding everything that symbolized the restrictions of the previous century: corsets, toe shoes, and Victorian morality went out. Free love, votes for women, and the automobile came in.

In that climate, simple art began to flourish in America. A young dancer, Ruth St. Denis—a contemporary of Isadora and of Fokine—succeeded in being taken seriously in her own country without the usual obligation of first proving herself abroad, mainly because she had a magnificent sense of theatre developed during her early years in lavishly spectacular Broadway shows. With this sound commercial background and a considerable ego, she set out to find artistic fulfillment.

One can say that, within the limitations of her field, Ruth St. Denis was an admirable artist. Her kind of kitsch, inspired originally by an advertisement for Egyptian cigarettes, was infused with a deeply sincere mystical conviction that made her a compelling performer, and undoubtedly she pioneered a public for serious dance with her Oriental fantasies set to Occidental music. One cannot say she explored new movements or motivations. She was no more modern than Isadora or Fokine.

The modern and contemporary dance that we know now is something absolutely new in the world in this century. It is the only dance form that comes from the intellect instead of, one way or another, through existing dance steps of ancient or peasant origin. The birth of modern dance occurred at roughly the same time Isadora was developing her seemingly new art, and partly because they both rejected classical ballet, they were confused in people's minds as one and the same thing. But it was in central Europe that the fountain of really original dance ideas was to be found—and they must have ranged from masterly to atrocious. The vogue for "eccentric" dances gave endless scope for the imagination, and if the results were sometimes bizarre, that only increases the entertainment value of photographs handed down from the period.

Probably among the most genuinely "modern" and tasteful of the many concert artists of that era were the three Wiesenthal sisters in Vienna. Grete Wiesenthal's choreography for a waltz in flowing evening gown, with champagne glass in hand, epitomized the liberated

RUTH ST. DENIS AS ALGERIAN DANCING GIRL, 1920

young woman of pre-World War I Europe. It was completely contemporary in 1907, and is still a very good work today because it remains a valid expression of its time. It is odd to realize that Wiesenthal was several years ahead of the first ballet in contemporary clothes presented by Serge Diaghilev. That was *Jeux* in 1913, but Diaghilev's Ballets Russes seasons in Paris, from 1909 onwards, overshadowed all other dance activity taking place in Europe, because apart from his own remarkable talents as an artistic director, the technical ability of his dancers gave him a tremendous advantage over most of the "modern" recitalists—even those who had excellent ideas and good taste lacked sufficient dancing skill to exploit them to the full.

The Sakharoffs, for example, were a couple whose work consisted of expressive numbers, magnificently costumed, which they described as "abstract pantomime." Alexander Sakharoff was born in Russia and went to Paris to study law and painting. He was so impressed by Sarah Bernhardt dancing a minuet in a play that he decided to become a dancer and, after a little acrobatic training, put together his first program in 1910. With that sparse technique, he and his attractive German wife, Clothilde, were able to make life-

THE WIESENTHAL SISTERS

long careers touring the world, but no one attaches much importance to them these days. One should remember, though, that for two dancers to hold the stage for an entire evening and send the audience home happy, as they consistently did, took a fair degree of artistic integrity and imagination; and they even succeeded in impressing Russia's reigning ballerina, Mathilde Kschessinskaya, who saw them in Paris. The Sakharoffs spread dance appreciation to audiences far and away beyond the reach of a large company like the Diaghilev ballet, and that was a very important function—for that matter, it still is.

Experimentation and innovation draw on many sources for inspiration and the theories of a quite extraordinary and fascinating Frenchman named François Delsarte lurk behind a great deal of modern dance. (It is curious that France, his own country, paid less attention to him than did America or Germany.) Delsarte was born in 1811. He must have been an engaging "nutty professor" of a man. He started out as an opera singer, but lost his voice,

THE ARTISTIC DANCE

HANSI DICHTL

LIESEL PINK-PANK

so he turned his attention instead to the meaningless gestures that passed for acting in his erstwhile profession, and decided to study natural human movement as it unconsciously expressed emotion. Each observation led him further, until twenty-five years had passed in the research phase alone. Yet another twenty-five years of collating and analyzing his notes left him convinced that his work was "too unfinished for publication," a remark I find irresistibly charming. He must have been laughable, hiding in shrubberies in the park with a notebook, observing the difference between a mother's attitude to her child and that of its nanny—even between the gestures of an adoring mother and an indifferent one. As he studied people in cafés and churches, in mourning and in anger, in rejoicing and in anxiety, he was able to formulate precise laws governing our every unconscious movement that enabled him to read character, emotions, and motives infallibly and in great detail. I believe his was the first scientific approach to human expression through body movement.

The next important researcher, also a non-dancer, was Emile Jaques-Dalcroze, a

THE ARTISTIC DANCE

LYSANA   WALTER JUNK

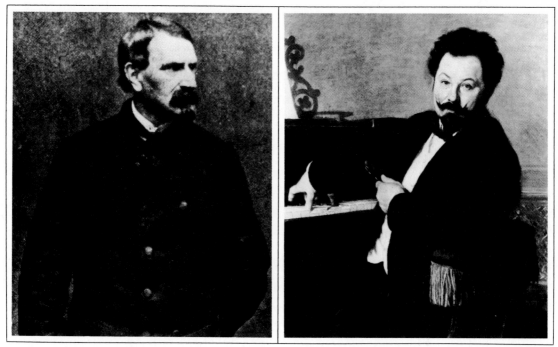

Swiss musician born in Vienna in 1865. Delsarte had wanted to make singers act better; Dalcroze wanted to make musicians more musical, and he devised a combination of rhythm and gymnastics that he called eurythmics. The fact that he attracted so many dancers to his schools in Germany and Switzerland was a real sign of the times; he never pretended to teach dance, but translated crotchets and quavers into physical terms. It was enough for his students to walk, run, and wave their arms to convince most people that his was a school of dancing.

The person who ultimately related this type of study most closely to genuine dance was a strange, colourful giant of a man named Rudolf von Laban—or just Rudolf Laban—

EXERCISE IN RHYTHMIQUES: "BEATING ¦ IN CANON WITH EXPRESSION"

GYMNASTIQUE RHYTHMIQUE

born in Bratislava in 1879, the son of an army general. He was over six feet tall, well built, wore an Assyrian beard, and made the most of his magnetic attraction for women—"his inescapable charm." In his teens, Laban saw dervishes perform their whirling dance that is used to induce religious trances. He was instantly intrigued by the idea of a spiritual purpose for dancing, and his fascination with the other possible applications of such movement lasted the rest of his life.

It is unlikely that a mind as enquiring, progressive, and analytical as his had ever before focussed so acutely on the mysteries of human movement. The field was wide open, but he was far too restless and impulsive to follow anything to its conclusion himself—excepting only his system of movement-notation. He always left others to cultivate the ground while he rushed ahead indicating new paths for research as he moved between Germany, Italy, and Switzerland teaching dance, eurythmics, and "personality cult." Progressive art groups gathered around him wherever he went. Eventually, he settled in England, where war-time factory workers benefitted from his studies of labour-saving movement on the production line, and school children in dancing class were encouraged to run about in bare feet improvising self-expression.

I do not believe his choreography or dance teaching had much merit in themselves; and yet it was his approach to movement as existing creatively and expressively on its own, with or without music, décor, or costume, and his association of dance with psychology, philosophy, mysticism, and cosmology that is the basis of modern and contemporary dance. He was the focal point for central European dance, a very significant style in which his pupil Mary Wigman was the prime force.

This new dancing differed radically from Isadora Duncan's aesthetic principle. Isadora could never have made use of a deliberately ugly movement, least of all an unfeminine one, whereas Mary Wigman cultivated, if not a masculine strength, at least a strong unisex style and personality. She was the dedicated pioneer of a type of dance that owed nothing to the past. It expressed the twentieth-century psychology, the burning desire for self-awareness and individual freedom of expression, unfettered, harsh, and real; and it was born in the mind.

In 1914 the beginning of World War I disrupted Europe and, among other more essential things, its modern dance. In the same year, in America, Ruth St. Denis married a serious and ambitious young man named Ted Shawn. Their partnership was to give modern dance its American springboard.

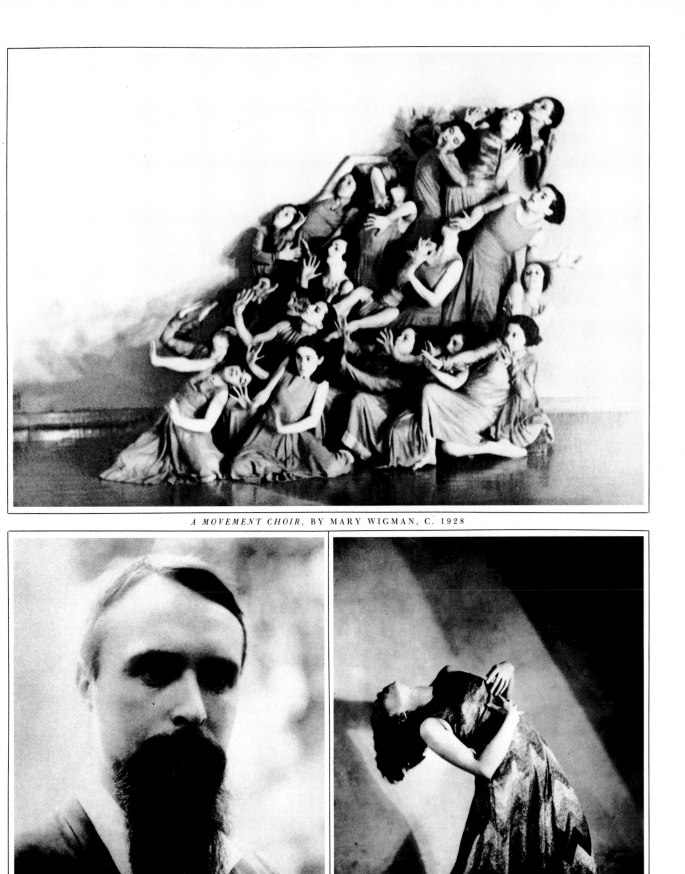

A MOVEMENT CHOIR, BY MARY WIGMAN, C. 1928

RUDOLF VON LABAN

MARY WIGMAN IN HER *DANCE OF SORROWS*

RUTH ST. DENIS AND TED SHAWN

Ted Shawn was never a great dancer—it was difficult for anyone to become a serious dancer at all in America at that time—but his choreography was exceptional by current standards, and he had a flair for mixing art and business in the right proportions, cleverly devising programs that allowed St. Denis her mystic vein but ended with a dash of ragtime jazz. The public loved it, but their marriage didn't last. Neither of them had much sense of humour regarding themselves, and St. Denis never appreciated Shawn's greater intelligence: it was he who realized they should open a school, both to consolidate their art and as an umbrella against the rainy days of the theatre business. Someone coined the name Denishawn, and it caught on. By shrewdly making sure that Denishawn was synonymous in the public mind with art and good taste, Shawn provided an ambiance in which America's real "Mother of Modern Dance," Martha Graham, was able to discover her own direction.

Graham was influenced by the stage personality of St. Denis and by the clever choreographer and theorist that was Ted Shawn, but when she emerged from their school she already had a very definite mind of her own. Their assortment of dance styles, includ-

UTH ST. DENIS EXOTICA—EGYPTIAN, MEXICAN, EASTERN WITH TED SHAWN, JAPANESE WITH CHARLES WEIDMAN

TED SHAWN AND HIS MEN DANCERS

ing ballet, didn't satisfy her intellectually. She could have chosen Mary Wigman's path of intense, concentrated, bare presentations, so pared down to the pure essence of personal expression that they appealed only to a very serious and dedicated audience. Instead, Graham—no less intense as an artist—presented her dance in terms of theatre, where theme, music, colour, and movement are partners. But she did not accept that the dancer, in whatever role and whatever appropriate setting, merely interprets the music like an instrument of the orchestra. The Graham dancer has a personal statement to make in movement, for which music and design must be integrated to the dance. To achieve this, she commissioned music that was as contemporary as her choreographic conception, and she chose artists, sculptors, and architects who saw theatre design not as pictures but as forms in space.

Most important of all was her own star quality. Her striking appearance and domination of the stage, her dramatic power as dancer-actress, and her intense involvement

DORIS HUMPHREY AND CHARLES WEIDMAN, C. 1942

would have made her a star in whatever branch of theatre she chose. Her intelligence enabled her to make a new style of movement conform to the laws of theatre without sacrificing integrity.

Martha Graham's secret seems to lie in her combination of emotion and intellect, of feminine and masculine—the feminine star with masculine creativity—and her combination of egocentric artist with unselfish pedagogue. She knew how to give modern dance its own vocabulary of movement, its own technique, making it a coherent art form in the middle of isolated individual experiments. Some of those individual efforts have grown into little dynasties—notably that of Doris Humphrey, another Denishawn pupil. But

MARTHA GRAHAM

IN 1937

AS MEDEA IN *CAVE OF THE HEART*

WITH HER COMPANY IN *PRIMITIVE MYSTERIES*

MARTHA GRAHAM, MAY O'DONNELL, MERCE CUNNINGHAM, AND ERICK HAWKINS IN *APPALACHIAN SPRING*

although Graham's school is the necessary central force of modern dance, there is always room for original creation. The astonishing thing is that Martha Graham, now in her eighties, is still alert, active, and creative, her timeless wisdom unimpaired. Undoubtedly she is the only one who merits the title "Mother of Modern Dance." The "Fathers" were in central Europe.

When we look back more than sixty-five years, the strangest fact of all—which in no way detracts from the "Parents," because it was a single incident—is that the first truly modern ballet, conceived intellectually without conforming to any prior dance aesthetics, was

created not by a figure associated with modern dance itself but by the most famous of ballet dancers, Vaslav Nijinsky. In 1913, when he choreographed *The Rite of Spring*, he suddenly and inexplicably invented a new idiom that cut straight to the heart of modern dance. This extraordinary ballet was first performed a year before Mary Wigman made her début, and long before Rudolf Laban devised his system of movement-notation which could have recorded the choreography. Unfortunately, Nijinsky's complex marriage of steps to Stravinsky's powerful music was almost incomprehensible to the dancers, so it did not remain long in their memories—most of them, with their inflexible ballet minds, hated it anyway. Marie Rambert, a Dalcroze student who helped Nijinsky analyze the musical phrasing, and was also one of the performers, still recalls the long hours of work involved, but naturally doesn't remember the choreography; and Nijinsky lost his reason a few years after its creation. So the original *Rite* is irretrievable. It has long since passed into legend, but the unprecedented scandal of its première in Paris is recorded by many who were present: a young artist, Mlle. Valentine Gross, who thought the ballet "astoundingly beautiful," described the performance:

> *Nothing that has ever been written about the battle of* Le Sacre du Printemps *has given a faint idea of what actually took place. The theatre seemed to be shaken by an earthquake. It seemed to shudder. People shouted insults, howled and whistled, drowning the music. There was slapping and even punching. Words are inadequate to describe such a scene. . . . I cannot think how it was possible for this ballet, which the public of 1913 found so difficult, to be danced through to the end in such an uproar. The dancers could not hear the music. . . . Diaghilev thundered orders from his box. . . .*

We will never be able to see Nijinsky's "astoundingly beautiful" sensation, never be able to judge for ourselves or know what impact the "earthquake" would make on us. All we know is that *The Rite of Spring* was created before modern dance saw the light of day; that its movements were totally in opposition to ballet; and that Isadora Duncan was doing a few simple skips and steps for which she is credited with inspiring modern dance, while Nijinsky, the brilliant innovator whose masterpiece is unrecorded, suffers the irony of going down in history as the spirit of a perfumed rose. His famous leap through the window in *Le Spectre de la Rose* will always overshadow his leap ahead of other choreographers into an unexplored area of movement.

PAUL TAYLOR WITH BETTY DE JONG

MERCE CUNNINGHAM

TWYLA THARP (*RIGHT*) AND COMPANY

DANCE IMPERIAL

I desire that my message of beauty and joy
and life shall be taken up and carried on after me.
I hope that when Anna Pavlova is forgotten the memory
of her dancing will live with the people.
If I have achieved even that little for my art I am content.

—ANNA PAVLOVA

Anna Pavlova, the greatest dancer the world has ever known! How is it possible to explain genius? Genius is another word for magic, and the whole point of magic is that it is inexplicable.

There was nothing in Pavlova's background to suggest she might become a great ballerina. She did not come from one of the old ballet clans whose children grew up in the atmosphere of the profession, among parents, uncles, and aunts who were all on the stage. Her most illustrious predecessor in the ballet, Marie Taglioni, who died as a very old lady when Pavlova was three, was the daughter, niece, sister, and aunt of other dancers, but Pavlova was an only child and her parents were not connected with the theatre. She was a unique phenomenon, without explanation, like the evening star or the Chinese flower that blooms only once in a hundred years.

If one goes by the rules, Pavlova's technique was not absolutely pure and correct—although she did certain steps with a brilliance unequalled by anyone since. But what was supreme was her ability to transform herself into whatever she chose: a flower, a swan, a dragonfly, or just charm and gaiety incarnate. Her movements forgot classroom rules as her entire being took on the essence of a role, using only a few runs, a few poses, and an arabesque to make a miracle. That was Pavlova's magic.

PAVLOVA AGED 9

PAVLOVA'S CHILDHOOD HOME AT LIGOVO   AT 15

She was born in St. Petersburg in 1881, a premature baby and very frail. Her father died when she was two, leaving her mother extremely poor, so Anna spent most of her childhood at Ligovo, a small village outside St. Petersburg, with her grandmother. She was eight when her mother took her, as a Christmas treat, to see *The Sleeping Beauty* at the Maryinsky Theatre, and from that moment on she could think only of dancing. But she had to contain her excitement for two years until she reached the age to audition at the ballet school. So began Pavlova's life and career—for they were one and the same thing.

All her life she remained slender and fragile-looking, with an unusually long neck, an oval face, and highly arched insteps that added a particular beauty to the line of her legs and feet. She graduated from the ballet school to the stage of the Maryinsky Theatre, to be quickly picked out as a future star by the discriminating habitués, a small public made up almost exclusively of ultra-conservative court officials and high-born families. They were passionately enthusiastic about their favourite artists; after Marie Taglioni's last performance in St. Petersburg some sixty years earlier, the audience was so ecstatic that her flimsy ballet slipper was cooked by a chef—in a rich sauce I hope—and eaten by her most fanatical admirers. She was showered with jewels and furs and left Russia with a fortune.

As one of the Czar's Imperial Theatres, supported out of his personal budget, the Maryinsky was in essence part of the Imperial household, and the artists were Imperial ser-

vants. To make any change in routine, such as an early retirement, a petition had to be sent to the Czar for approval. But the theatre and theatre schools were generously subsidized, and a ballerina such as Pavlova was almost like a hothouse plant, brought to flower in an atmosphere of revered traditions and displayed in the perfect setting of the finest ballet company in the world. Few dancers left that security and comfort except in the summer, while the theatre in St. Petersburg was closed, when they might make short tours. It is impossible to know just when or why Pavlova first felt the compulsion to break away from that ideal setting to take the beauty of dance to the farthermost corners of the world. She must have grown up among lingering memories of the legendary Taglioni, and perhaps she always cherished the story of Taglioni's travels and triumphs all over Europe.

In any event, on Pavlova's first trip abroad, to Stockholm, her dancing caused such a sensation that after the performance young men took the horses from the shafts of her carriage and drew it back to the hotel themselves. In the nineteenth century this charming tribute had been paid to only one or two ballerinas, and it must have been exhilarating for the young Pavlova to be accorded such a quaint, old-fashioned compliment in 1908.

By this time she had overcome the inherent physical weaknesses of her childhood by submitting herself to gruelling coaching, four years in all, first with a retired ballerina and then with the most famous teacher of the Milan school, Enrico Cecchetti. She en-

THE BUTTERFLY

THE DRAGONFLY

LA FILLE MAL GARDÉE

AUTUMN LEAVES WITH AUBREY HITCHENS

RONDINO

GAVOTTE

THE DYING SWAN

ORIENTAL IMPRESSIONS WITH UDAY SHANKAR

WITH HER BOSTON TERRIER

gaged him to work exclusively with her until she gained enough strength and endurance to triumph in all the ballerina test pieces—the classical repertoire of Marius Petipa. In 1912, married, secure, and approaching the height of her powers, and having tasted life outside the periphery of the Czar's Imperial Theatre, Pavlova and her husband bought a house—the only home she was to have for the rest of her life—not in St. Petersburg, but in

WITH HER PET SWAN, JACK

London on Hampstead Hill. One would love to know why they chose London rather than Paris. French was the court language in St. Petersburg and Russians normally gravitated to France as their second country, but Pavlova bought and loved Ivy House, with its sloping garden, old trees, and a pond for the swans—with which she had such an affinity. I think the happiest moments of her life must have been spent there. Certainly, the only

photographs that give an insight into her life and personality as a woman, rather than as a dancer, are the ones in her garden and house with her husband, surrounded by her pets, for she adored all animals and birds.

She was so constantly immersed in dance that she leaves few traces that are not manifestly more artist than woman. One knows more about her life in the theatre than out; for example, she was demanding of those who worked with her, but much more so of herself, and followed a schedule that few could match. When everyone was suffering in tropical temperatures, she would say, "What a marvellous climate for dancing, it is so easy to warm up!" When it was cold, she said she found it bracing. In her rare free moments, she taught a few selected pupils or sculpted the delicate figurines that give such a clear picture of herself in motion. *Everything* she did seemed directly related to dance. Even if she was only posing for snapshots in ordinary dresses (though never really ordinary if she wore

AT THE HAMBURG ZOO TEACHING AN ARABESQUE

them), and especially in hats or evening gowns, Pavlova was elegant and beautiful, but in a manner that was different from other women.

In 1912, when she and her husband bought Ivy House, it was like a bird testing its wings, for two years later she formed her own ballet company with all the difficulties and responsibilities that entailed. Nothing could have been more taxing, and it seems extraordinary that someone who could have shone like the most precious diamond in an Imperial tiara would relinquish that favoured position so easily. Pavlova also had the opportunity to

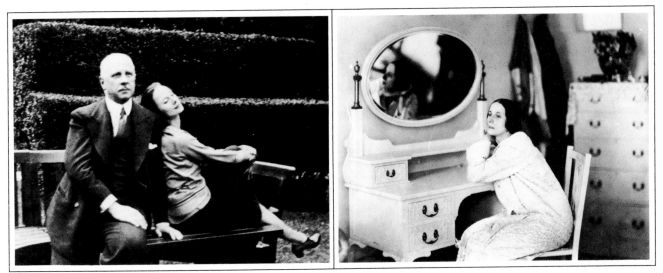

WITH HER HUSBAND, VICTOR DANDRÉ, AND IN HER DRESSING ROOM

lead Diaghilev's ballet, and it would have been an easier way of life for her, but they could never have worked together because they were destined to serve different ends: Diaghilev to change the course of dance aesthetics, and she to take ballet to the world. Undoubtedly Pavlova felt herself and her life ruled by a mission. She had to dance for everyone, everywhere in the world; no town was too small, no stage too humble. And no one who saw her ever forgot the experience of her art; the memory of it flickers as long as there are still people alive who can tell us of her magic.

She danced in Russia for the last time in 1914. Some seventeen years and three hundred thousand miles later she was about to embark on a farewell tour of Europe when she caught a chill and died of pleurisy in The Hague. It is said that her last words were to ask for her swan costume to be prepared. The cremation took place in London near her beloved home, which she had so rarely been able to enjoy. Although it will soon be fifty years since that bleak day when the world lost its supreme artist of dance, a memorial service held each year in the Russian Orthodox Church in London still draws old friends and many admirers far too young ever to have seen her dance.

I believe the qualities that set her above all other dancers were an intensity of spirit, a passionate compulsion, and a grace that made every tiny movement significant; where others have to learn their art, hers burst forth like the heat of the sun. I believe that without dance she would have been incomplete, and certainly dance without Pavlova would be incomplete.

It was Russia, and the traditions and training of Russian ballet, that produced this miracle—for Russia is where ballet was then at its height—but the seeds had been carried from France and cultivated by French ballet masters ever since the seventeenth century, when Louix XIV issued the decree that gave birth to ballet as a theatre art. Seen from Europe in those distant times, Russia was a vast, semi-barbaric expanse, while America was an immense, partly colonized wilderness. Now they are the two superpowers of the world, and since the time of the Sun King, the creative centre of ballet has travelled first to one and then to the other; from France to Russia and from Russia to America.

It is understandable that ballet should have taken root and flourished so successfully in Russia, because it found there such a richness of national dance to feed on. Russia is unique in that the two most ancient and basic types of folk dance, the Oriental and the European, converge on its border states. All Oriental dance forms originated in India, from where they spread to Southeast Asia, the Philippines, and as far as China and Japan; while to the west, their influence travelled through the Middle East and southern Europe to Spain. Obviously Russia is closest to the centre of this vital influence and also to the very distinctive folk dances of all central Europe; and, of course, in Russia itself even the bears dance!

The first move towards developing Russian ballet came late in the seventeenth century when news of the grandiose entertainments fashionable in the courts of western Europe tempted Czar Alexei to order his own presentation of "French dancing," as he described it. In those days all such entertainments were made up of speech, music, and dance, none of which was stinted. The Czar was enthralled through all ten hours of the first presentation, which his courtiers miraculously had prepared in barely two weeks.

Sometime later, the Empress Anna Ivanovna gave an evening of opera, ending in a danced scene which is recorded as the first ballet presented in Russia. It couldn't have been as we would imagine, for it was danced by more than one hundred military cadets—the sons of noble families, naturally—and there is no mention of any girls taking part. The most important person involved was undoubtedly the French ballet master Jean-Baptiste Landé, who had trained the cadets for two years prior to the performance and subsequently was granted permission to found a ballet school. Thus, less than seventy years after Louis XIV founded professional ballet in 1669 in Paris, St. Petersburg opened its school in 1738 in a wing of the royal palace, with twenty-four children of Imperial retainers. It developed into the school that produced Anna Pavlova and is still the most prestigious of all ballet academies, now attached to the Kirov Theatre in Leningrad. Moscow followed soon after with its own school set up in an orphanage.

Peter the Great, who became Czar in 1689, was passionately fond of every kind of party and masquerade and introduced the latest ballroom dances from the Western capitals, making it an obligatory social accomplishment to dance well. By the end of the seventeenth century, dance had become part of the life at all levels of society—peasant, aristocrat, and theatre professional. There were also the serf artists—actors, dancers, and musicians who, if they were lucky, were given excellent training by foreign masters. The enlightened Count Sheremetiev, for example, whose house is now a fascinating museum containing its own theatre, engaged, among others, a famous French dancer and master, Charles Le Picq (nicknamed the "Apollo of Dance"), to bring his private ballet to professional levels. His dancers, being serfs, could be sold without so much as a by-your-leave, and many were purchased by the commercial, and even the Imperial, theatre managements in Moscow. The last such sale took place in 1806.

"EVEN THE BEARS DANCED!"

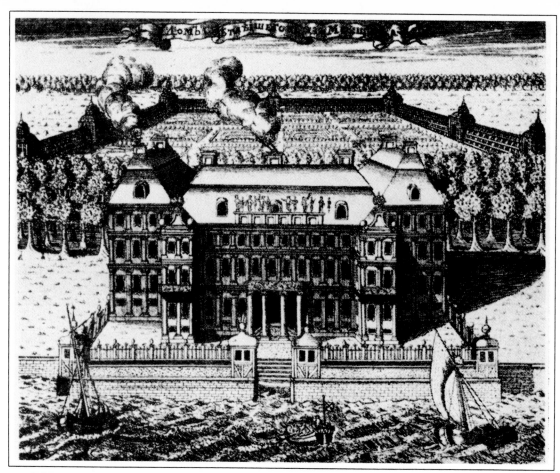

THE ROYAL PALACE, ST. PETERSBURG, SITE OF THE FIRST RUSSIAN BALLET SCHOOL

The importation of foreign ballet masters to direct and develop Russia's ballet was fairly consistent for two hundred years. And the selection of those talents, whether by accident or design, was brilliant. Of the nineteenth-century travellers, the one I find most endearing is Charles-Louis Didelot. He was such a lively little man, and extremely important for Russia as an innovator who led ballet in new directions. Outside the theatre he was very soft-hearted, but on the job, according to this description of him in his later years, he was a strict disciplinarian, one of the old breed of ballet masters:

> *It was very amusing to see Didelot behind the scenes watching his pupils. Sometimes he swayed from side to side, smiled, and took mincing steps and stamped his foot. But when the little pupils danced he shook his fist at them, and if they missed the figures he made their lives a misery. He pounced on them like a hawk, pulled their hair or ears, and, if any ran away, he gave them a kick which sent them flying. Even the solo dancers suffered from him. Being applauded, a dancer went behind the scenes, where Didelot seized her by the shoulders, shook her with all his might, and giving her a punch in the back, pushed her on to the stage as if she were recalled.*

CHARLES-LOUIS DIDELOT

In spite of this he was deeply loved by all, because they knew how much he cared for perfection.

Didelot was born in Stockholm, where his father was engaged as principal dancer at the Royal Theatre. When he caught smallpox at the age of six, his face was so badly scarred that his father thought he could never go on the stage. Then fate intervened in a most unusual way. The king's brother wanted to take his pet marmot with him to a masked ball, but as the animal could not be found at the last moment, little Didelot was substituted, wearing a squirrel-fur outfit; and he played his part so comically all evening that the king was quite taken with his lively talent and sent him to Paris for ballet training. He was very bright and became an excellent dancer, although his appearance was always against him. He was described as a thin skeleton with a long red nose.

As a choreographer and teacher his success was enormous. His beautiful groupings were praised as immensely imaginative, and the poet Pushkin described them as having "an amazing charm," but his greatest coup de théâtre was to introduce realistic flying by individual dancers on almost invisible wires.

The public had become rather bored with the obviousness of the little platforms

MME. SACCHI, TIGHTROPE WALKER, AT COVENT GARDEN, C. 1816

ANTOINE PAUL AS ZÉPHYR

(called gloires) hung on heavy ropes that carried performers up and down from the heavens amid cardboard clouds. Even though the Italians had perfected very convincing cotton-wool clouds, nothing could compare with the beauty and thrill of Didelot's dancers as they took off into the air on a whim and apparently unaided.

His first "flying ballet" was seen in 1796 in London, which was then a real hive of ballet activity. When Zéphyr, in *Zéphyr Inconstant,* took lightly to the skies to escape an inconvenient mistress, the audience was astounded and rapturous, and some, no doubt, were envious. Of course the critics were alarmed, and predicted dire tragedies, but no one paid attention to them, and Didelot continued with ever more inventive use of these flying devices, matching whole groups on the stage with others in the air, and sending flights from side to side or from the back to the very edge of the footlights. He was perpetually at work seeking new scenarios, designing costumes, inventing machinery for new effects, creating choreographies, and teaching the dancers. He must have been a dynamo of energy and impatience. No wonder he had such a hot temper!

Didelot had not especially wanted to go to Russia; it was more to fill in time that he made his initial visit to St. Petersburg in 1801. Like all French ballet masters, he was set on producing his works at the Paris Opera. However, he was rebuffed by the management and conspired against by the two Gardel brothers (aided by their relations), who between them directed the ballet there for forty years; and he found in the Russian Imperial Theatre such a congenial atmosphere for work that he settled down for good and ended his days in retirement in Kiev. He was a great loss to France and a corresponding prize for Russia. It is said that the history of Russian choreography can be divided into two periods—before and after Didelot. He died in Kiev in 1837.

SELF-PORTRAITS BY JOHN DURANG: THE HORNPIPE   PAS SEUL À VESTRIS

The magical deceptions of stage machinery were an integral part of theatre throughout the eighteenth and nineteenth centuries. In this respect there was not such a chasm as exists now between the popular entertainment of the circus or music hall and pure ballet, where choreography has advanced so far that it is often sufficient unto itself. In Didelot's day, a choreographer had to capture his audience with good theatrical fare—a story, scenery, trick effects; everything magical. And Didelot knew very well how to do this; at the same time he was educating people to appreciate higher standards of dancing.

He had an exact contemporary in America who, with equal opportunties, might have rivalled his talents, for John Durang, who was born in Pennsylvania in 1768, was remarkably like Didelot in many ways: energetic, imaginative, resourceful, and he loved dancing. But no one sent Durang to study ballet in Paris, and there were no teachers in America. Nevertheless, he can fairly be called America's first dancer, and he must have been an attractive character from early youth, when (as he described himself) he was "active, industrious, full of health and cheerfulness." He was also as quick as a monkey; he could pick up any dance without lessons and play several instruments. He was about four-

THE HIGHLAND FLING   HARLEQUIN

teen when he saw a Frenchman named Roussel doing a hornpipe

> *which charmed my mind. I thought I could dance as well as anybody, but his style set it off, with his dress. I practised at home and I could soon do all his steps besides many more better Hornpipe steps. The pidgeon-wing I never saw done by any other person and I could not make that out from the front of the house. I contrived to get Mr. Roussel to board at my father's house that I might have the opportunity to dance more correct than I had been used to. The pidgeon was the only difficulty I had to encounter: he could not show me the principle and the anatomy of the figure of the step, nor I never met a dancer since that could have shown it to me. The mystery of the figure occurred to me in bed for my thoughts were constant on that object. I dream'd that I was at a ball and did the pidgeon-wing to the admiration of the whole company; in the morning I rose in confidence of doing the step.*

And so he did, and he was able to analyze it so effectively that he "never failed in teaching it and make my pupils master of it." Which shows that, untutored as he was, he had a true ballet master's mind.

GEORGE WASHINGTON SMITH

At seventeen he got his first stage engagement to dance his hornpipe. The audition, which took place on the morning of his début, found him victim of a paralyzing attack of nerves, but absolutely determined to win his public. So, never at a loss where theatre was concerned, he contrived a trampoline in the wings from which he made a flying entrance, landing bang in the middle of the stage and starting his dance amid bursts of applause. The audience, in an uproar, threw fruit and other tributes at the stage until the curtain was raised again and he repeated the dance. It was a good send-off to his career, which of necessity could hardly be confined to dance, for there were no ballet companies and, in any case, he could never resist an opportunity to present any form of entertainment that would give the public good value for their money. He could turn his hand as easily to acting, singing, pantomime, harlequinade, tightrope dancing, clowning on horseback, or jumping through a barrel of fire. What a man! And how he would have loved Didelot's flying ballets and all the sophisticated machinery of European stages.

In his time, Durang was rated by a fellow player as the best dancer in America, and George Washington, who was a very keen dancer in the ballroom, went repeatedly to

MARY ANN LEE, AGED 13

watch him at the South Street Theatre in Philadelphia, so I feel sure he had magic—and, anyway, who could resist the hero of this tale, which was only one of his many hair-raising adventures? ". . . One night as I was riding Cornplanter in a suit of armour with a visor on my face and in full speed with a shower of fireworks on the top of my helmet ending with an explosion, the explosion frightened the horse. He jumped over three benches of the pit, tore away a partition with his hind leg and landed in the passage at the stable door, and flung me over the orchestra on to the stage without any hurt to myself or horse." Very likely, after all that, he threw in a little hornpipe to re-assure the audience.

In the course of Durang's career, the United States saw an influx of dancers from Europe, beginning with émigrés from the French Revolution. Although none of them was extraordinary—except perhaps Monsieur and Madame Placide, because they somehow managed to dance ballet on a tightrope—their cumulative activities over a period of years improved the climate for dance in America.

During the American Revolution, when Durang was growing up, many people thought any kind of entertainment was positively wicked (unlike the French Revolution-

AUGUSTA MAYWOOD, AGED 12, IN *LE DIEU ET LA BAYADÈRE*

AUGUSTA MAYWOOD

aries, who rushed out and danced in the streets) and they almost succeeded in closing theatres altogether—many performances were advertised as "lectures" to avoid being banned. The foreign dancers arriving in the aftermath of these prejudices brought a welcome breath of European culture and, more important, they opened dancing schools. As a consequence, a girl who was born in Philadelphia in 1823, the year after John Durang's death, was able to become the first home-grown ballerina of the United States of America. She was Mary Ann Lee, who made an excellent success from the day of her début, aged fourteen, and she was the first American ballerina to dance *Giselle*. Her partner, George Washington Smith, was also a Philadelphian and for many years the only important American danseur; he had progressed successfully from clog dancing as a child to French classical ballet. Smith was lucky that his career struck at the right moment in America when ballet was getting off to a really good start, and before its European sources went into artistic decline, causing American ballet to wilt and die before it could build enough tradition to carry on alone. It had to bide its time, lying dormant like the Sleeping Beauty for one hundred years, until native talents could re-awaken and rise in full force.

Yet before going to sleep, it had time to send out its first international ballerina, Augusta Maywood. Only two years younger than Mary Ann Lee, she made a resoundingly successful job of conquering the old strongholds of Paris, Vienna, and Milan. This was an amazing feat when Paris was in the middle of a ballerina boom, and the courageous Augusta, at her Opera début, was not yet fifteen. Thanks to the critic Théophile Gautier, who never lets one down for a physical description of his subjects, I can picture her well with her "dark eyes, small features and eager untamed expression which verges on the beautiful." I have never heard of another dancer with "jaguar legs and the agility of a clown"—the combination boggles the mind—but the impression he gives of her in action makes her strong and bouncy, a bit brusque, almost aggressive and lacking grace, but very attractive nevertheless. (To make an obscure parallel, she could have been as original, within the narrow limits of Paris Opera novelties, as Twyla Tharp is in modern ballet, for she had her own very unusual manner and a surprising assurance that captivated the audience.)

Augusta was a thoroughly modern woman. Since she had been a successful professional ballerina from the age of twelve, when she first appeared in Philadelphia, it was no wonder that at almost sixteen, enjoying the heady experience of a Paris triumph, she found it humiliating to be guarded night and day by her mother. She eloped with a dancer and from then on ran her life and career her own way, discarding husbands and lovers when they no longer held her interest—*they* never discarded *her*—and making an admirable career throughout Europe. She was full of good common sense and found it more practical to tour with her own company than to be at the mercy of whatever dancers and facilities might be available in the theatres she visited. She took the pioneering spirit from America back to Europe and never returned to the country of her birth.

If Augusta Maywood was a pioneer, Juba was a harbinger. Like Augusta, he went to Europe, never to return to America—not, unfortunately, by choice, but because he died in London when he was twenty-seven. The phenomenon of Juba was like a synthesis of all the jazz dance that was to come in the future, wrapped together and thrown into the world ahead of its time. As far as anyone knows, he was born the same year as Augusta, in 1825. He was, of course, black, presumed to be a free-born Negro; his real name was William Henry Lane, but that is of no consequence at all, he was *dance*, and might as well have been called just that. Where he came from no one knows, where his genius came from no one knows, but everyone who saw him was entranced by his unique movement, incredible precision, and superb grace. Grace is the essential attribute of those born to dance—Pavlova and Nijinsky had grace, and so did Juba.

Pictured in London's Vauxhall Gardens in 1848, with hands in pockets, knee up, and well-turned-out leg, he is a compact, well-proportioned little man, with an elegant head, high shiny boots, and joy in his casual, light movement. He was also a first-rate singer and excelled at playing the tambourine, but when it came to dance, "No one ever saw such mobility of muscles, such flexibility of joints, such boundings, such slidings, such gyrations, such toes and heelings, such backwardings and forwardings, such postur-

JUBA AT VAUXHALL GARDENS, LONDON, 1848

ings, such firmness of foot, such elasticity of tendon, such mutation of movement, such vigor, such variety, such natural grace, such powers of endurance."

What a picture that conjures up of natural, spontaneous dance! He danced for himself—anywhere. It could be on a stage or in a crush of people in the heat and rhythm of a dance hall. His life and his dancing were indistinguishable and inseparable. He was tireless, and when at last he wore himself out, he died.

This passage by a London critic, three years before his death, seems to me to penetrate his soul as nothing else:

There never was such a laugh as the laugh of Juba—there is in it the concentrated laugh of fifty comic pantomimes; it has no relation to the chuckle, and least of all to the famous horse laugh; not a bit of it—it is a laugh distinct, a laugh apart, a laugh by itself—clear, ringing, echoing, resonant, harmonious, full of rejoicing and mighty mirth and fervent fun; you may hear it like the continuous humming sound of nature, permeating in everywhere; it enters your heart and you laugh sympathetically, it creeps into your ear and clings to it. . . .

JULES PERROT IN *NATHALIE*

In London, at the same time as Juba, was an important choreographer, Jules Perrot, who at thirty-eight was no longer the brilliant dancer he had been in his early twenties, partnering Marie Taglioni at the Paris Opera. She had been annoyed with him for getting more applause than she did, so he left the theatre and was never able to regain a place there. In January 1848 he was in Milan with Augusta Maywood, and that summer he was in London, where his curiosity might have taken him to see the Negro wonder at Vauxhall Gardens. We will never know. At the end of that year he went to St. Petersburg and was the next French ballet master after Didelot to have a strong influence on Russian ballet.

There was an infinite distance between the dance of Juba and the classical ballet of

FAIRY BALLET BY PERROT

Perrot, and if Perrot did see Juba, he must initially have classified his dancing with the "grotesque" style that had always been a feature of ballet entertainments. Nevertheless, being a more modern thinker than his contemporaries or close successors, he is the only nineteenth-century choreographer who might have appreciated Juba's genius to the full.

Perrot was unlucky as a dancer because the "era of the ballerina" began when he was about seventeen and suddenly ambitious to join the ballet instead of the popular boulevard theatres where he had been brought up among acrobats and mimes. He went to study with the great Auguste Vestris and became, very possibly, as good as his illustrious teacher, but, as the incident with Marie Taglioni shows, it was no longer a time for male dancers. It is amusing to notice how after about 1837, so many ballet titles at the Paris Opera completely ignored the male protagonist. There was *La Sylphide* (no mention of James); and *Giselle* (nothing about Albrecht); and a long list of apparently single ladies: *Nathalie, Lady Henriette, Paquita, Betty, Stella, Gemma,* and more.

Because of this bias, and in spite of his excellence as a dancer, Perrot found more po-

CARLOTTA GRISI AND LUCIEN PETIPA IN *LA PÈRI*, 1843   CERRITO AND SAINT-LÉON IN *LA FILLE DE MARBRE*, 18

tential in his creative gift for choreography. Like Didelot, he was extremely imaginative, and whenever he had a chance he avoided the over-romantic subjects that were fashionable in his early years, choosing instead heavily dramatic scenarios like *Faust* and *The Hunchback of Notre Dame* (which he called *La Esmeralda*, another female title!). *La Esmeralda* was first performed in London without encountering any problems, but in St. Petersburg it caused a scandal at the Imperial Theatre because a priest and a captain were villains while the common folk were heroes. Perrot was forced to resign his position after eleven successful years in which he had greatly enhanced the dramatic as well as the technical standards of the St. Petersburg ballet.

Not unexpectedly the hardiest survivor of all the mid-nineteenth-century ballets is the one that comes down to us mainly in Perrot's version, namely *Giselle*. The ballet was created for Carlotta Grisi, with whom Perrot had fallen in love—because of her violet eyes—when working in Naples. He coached her, took her to Paris, and actually choreographed her dances for the première of *Giselle* at the Opera, although he had no official position and was given no credit on the program because the rest of the ballet was done by the resident ballet master, Jean Coralli. Perrot also married Carlotta, but that was a minor facet of their relationship—some say they were never married at all.

Giselle was first given in 1841, but after about twenty years it was dropped from the Paris repertoire and forgotten. It lived on in Russia to become a test piece for ballerinas, and partly for that reason the name of Carlotta Grisi, as its first interpreter, tends to overshadow that of her husband. But Jules Perrot made a far greater contribution to ballet, and the most erudite contemporary dance historian, Lincoln Kirstein, believes he was perhaps as great a creator as Marius Petipa, who is generally accepted as the master of nineteenth-century Russian ballet.

Marius Petipa was already one of the principal dancers in St. Petersburg when Perrot arrived in 1848, so they must have worked closely together during the eleven years Perrot was ballet master. After his withdrawal on account of *La Esmeralda*, another Frenchman took his place. He was Arthur Saint-Léon, an amusing man, remarkable for being as good a violinist as a dancer, and managing to be both simultaneously in his own ballet *The Devil's Violin*. In a lithograph—wearing a frock coat, short breeches, high-fronted shoes, with hair flying, a moustache, and the violin tucked under his chin—he looks a bit cluttered for dancing. Nevertheless, he was apparently a virtuoso in both fields, having made his début as a violinist at the age of thirteen in Stuttgart, where his father was ballet master, and as a dancer the following year. He was also an excellent choreographer. I imagine him as suave and urbane, very different from Perrot, the son of a stage carpenter. Perrot was inclined to be moody, and although probably far more original than Saint-Léon, had no idea how to be diplomatic when he wanted to get his own way.

Saint-Léon, like Perrot, had for a while a famous Italian ballerina wife, Fanny Cerrito. Unlike Perrot, he attained the coveted position of ballet master at the Paris Opera, which eluded so many other gifted French choreographers. It was there, in 1870, that he created the ballet *Coppélia*, his lasting achievement and still a great favourite. He was, incidentally, the only true Parisian among the great French ballet masters; he was born in the capital and died there of a heart attack when he was forty-nine. In his spare time, he had invented a system of dance notation and composed an occasional ballet score.

In 1862 it was finally the turn of Marius Petipa to become principal ballet master and choreographer of the Imperial ballet in St. Petersburg. Considering that he had created his first ballets when he was twenty, in France, it must have taken a lot of patience to wait until he was forty-four to be entrusted with that responsibility in Russia. When the opportunity came he was the proverbial right man in the right place at the right time to bring together

SAINT-LÉON IN *LA ESMERALDA*

MARIUS PETIPA

Russian dancers, French ballet training, European national dances, dramatic gesture, and stage spectacle, and tie them all together in a perfect knot for the Czar of all the Russias. Petipa was a tidy and methodical man.

Like so many of the great ballet masters of the past, he came of a dancing family. Temperamentally, he seems to have had more in common with his father, Jean-Antoine, than with his elder brother, Lucien, who was the best dancer of the three. Lucien was handsome, elegant, and very French, so he was extremely successful at the Paris Opera, where he partnered the greatest ballerinas of his day. He rarely travelled abroad and died no farther away from Paris than Versailles. Marius and his father were quite the opposite. Until they reached Russia, they were always on the move. As Jean-Antoine had married very young, he was still dancing when his sons were established in their careers, and he went off to New York in 1839 with the twenty-one-year-old Marius. But they soon returned. One can speculate on what might have happened to Russian ballet if they had decided to stay in America. Marius' creative genius would have remained largely unknown and frustrated for lack of suitably trained dancers, while ballet in Russia could have missed its golden moment or taken another course under the direction of Lev Ivanov, the man who was never able to rise beyond the position of Petipa's assistant.

Since Marius was the man most responsible for ballet reaching its ultimate heights in St. Petersburg, one might wonder why it was *that* city and not Paris—or any other Euro-

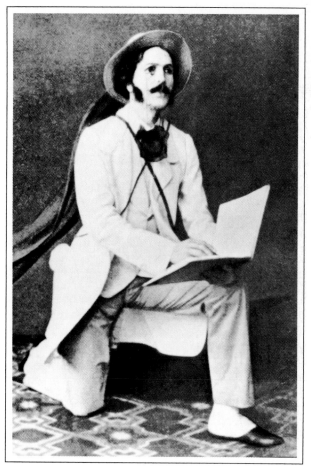

PETIPA AS LORD WILSON IN *PHARAOH'S DAUGHTER*

pean capital—which provided the appropriate ambiance. Briefly, Paris was neglecting the importance of male dancers and failing to recognize its best choreographers. London's more discerning theatre managers could offer no security of contract, as they ran unsubsidized commercial houses. Both Italy and Germany were divided into too many separate states for any one major capital to draw all the best talents together, while Copenhagen and Stockholm were conserving rather than developing their traditions. Vienna would have been the obvious place, but although it attracted the best Italian and Viennese choreographers and was periodically an important centre, there was never the steady progression of ballet masters, each building on the work of the last, which St. Petersburg adroitly engineered, thereby charming those who might have preferred to work elsewhere into remaining.

Even the Russian climate (Didelot had an allowance of firewood written into his contract) and the difficult overland journey (on which Marie Taglioni was held up by a famous bandit and compelled to dance on fur rugs spread over the muddy road or else forfeit her money and jewels) were compensated for by other factors, including the excellent contracts and the long annual vacations. Another was the attitude of Russian dancers to

PETIPA AS TA-HOR IN *PHARAOH'S DAUGHTER*

PETIPA WITH HIS SON AND DAUGHTER

their art. In any country, good dancers will spring up like well-watered flowers if they are inspired by good leadership, but the capacity of Russian dancers for total involvement in their work is not easily found elsewhere. A French critic visiting Russia in 1858 was amazed that the ladies of the corps de ballet did not "giggle, talk or leer at the public."

Jean-Antoine and Marius Petipa reached St. Petersburg towards the end of the 1840's and put down roots. Fate had decreed that they were both to see out their lives far from their homeland—not in America, which was nowhere near ready to receive the choreographer of the century, nor in Spain, where they had been enamoured of the irresistible rhythms and spirited dances (and of the ladies, too, so far as bachelor Marius was concerned), but in Russia. Marius was to have two Russian wives and several children, and he lived until he was ninety-two.

In his youth he was a neat man with observant, bright eyes. I am sure his movements and speech were precise, his mind well ordered and always busy. Choreographers have different ways of working, some creating their designs step by step with the dancers in rehearsal. Petipa's ballets were thoroughly planned at home before he arrived at the studio to put into operation the movement of his large numbers of dancers. He divided his corps de ballet into groups that wheeled and circled, crisscrossed and formed lines and chains in a gloriously inevitable flow that settled into a harmonious picture with the last chord of music. He was particularly preoccupied with the limitations of human stature, and broke the uniform height line of his moving body of dancers in the most ingenious ways to arrive at pictorially satisfying compositions. For one thing, he frequently introduced children in lines and patterns that intertwined with the adults, and he contrasted lying, kneeling, half-lunge, and full-pointe positions whenever the dancers came to rest, to create a pyramid.

He also made use of a tremendous variety of props such as garlands, scarfs, baskets of flowers, wands, ribbons, and little stools that some of the dancers carried to stand on at certain moments in the choreography—adding extra height. His most extraordinary flight of fancy was a "Dance of the Caryatides"; the corps de ballet, both men and women, carried baskets on their heads, baskets which, at the dénouement, disgorged, each one, a little child—a *very* little child, I would say.

I well remember that in our English production of *The Sleeping Beauty* in 1939, taken from the Maryinsky original, there was a moment in Act II when a model rock about twelve inches high was dragged onto the stage by the corps de ballet. It had a special toehold into which I had to place my foot and balance for a moment on pointe, the focal peak

THE SLEEPING BEAUTY, C. 1890

THE NUTCRACKER, 1892

SWAN LAKE

SWAN LAKE WITH PAVEL GERDT, 1895

of a carefully arranged group of nymphs. There is an 1840 lithograph of Marie Taglioni poised in such a way on a flower, so all those devices were well established in Petipa's youth, before ballerinas were ever lifted by their partners. It was not surprising that he was the one most intent on exploring the possibilities of elevating the ladies gracefully in the arms of their stalwart partners, even to sit on their shoulders.

Thus was born the modern pas de deux. Goodness knows what Petipa would think if he could see some of the contortions it has led to in these permissive days! It would have been unthinkable to him to see a ballerina upside down. A ballerina had to look her prettiest and most fashionable, bedecked with jewels, wearing a knee-length tutu skirt, and combining dignity with utmost charm. His star ballerina, Mathilde Kschessinskaya, was the most fascinating and fashionable of this entire period, and she had plenty of real jewels with which to adorn her radiant person on or off the stage. She was coquettish, amusing, vivacious, enchanting, and lived a life more fantastic than a fairy tale.

She was a romantic from the start. Customarily, the Czar and his family visited the Imperial Ballet School once a year at graduation, which was followed by a supper. On this occasion, Kschessinskaya, as one of the top graduates, found herself sitting next to the

THE NUTCRACKER WITH GERDT AND V. A. NIKITINA, 1892

MARIE TAGLIONI (POISED ON A TOEHOLD) AND ANTONIO GUERRA IN *L'OMBRE*

MATHILDE KSCHESSINSKAYA

Czarevitch, who was to become Nicholas II, the last Czar of Russia. She promptly fell in love, and very soon bewitched the young man who provided her with a modest but comfortable home where they could enjoy their idyll. The house saw parties, singing, champagne, and all the mad gaiety of youth—a life she returned to blithely as soon as she was able to surmount the terrible emotion caused by her prince's love match with golden-haired Princess Alix of Hesse-Darmstadt, the last Czarina. The future Czar thoughtfully gave Kschessinskaya their house as a farewell present—she already had quite a few jewels. She was never to meet her "beloved Niki" again. Instead, the Grand Duke Serge Mikhailovitch took care of her, and added a lovely country retreat to the comforts of her life.

The birth of her son by André, another Grand Duke (whom she eventually married in exile), was difficult to explain away to her protector, Serge Mikhailovitch. But the dear man was charming about it, and maintained his concern for her every wish so that, in the Imperial cauldron of intrigue that was the Maryinsky Theatre, she was someone to be reckoned with. Everyone knew that, as a last resort, she could and would send a request to the Czar. She was spoiled—my goodness!—and capricious, seeing slights and intended plots against her everywhere, yet she was also warm-hearted and generous to a degree, and

KSCHESSINSKAYA WITH HER FATHER

courageous; in later years, she never uttered a word of complaint about her drastically changed fortunes.

In spite of being so swamped in luxuries, she could not have been more conscientious in her work. No matter that none of her lovers was less than a grand duke, she was first and foremost a dancer—the daughter of Felix Kschessinsky, a fine character dancer—a ballerina who had passed through the Imperial Ballet School and earned her position as prima ballerina assoluta on the Maryinsky stage, where she sparkled like the genuine diamonds in her hair.

In the year of her graduation, 1890, Petipa's *Sleeping Beauty* had its première with an Italian ballerina, Carlotta Brianza. Probably Kschessinskaya decided then and there to prove that Russian dancers could do anything Italian ballerinas could do, because she was the first to tackle and master some of the most technically difficult steps developed and taught only in Milan. It had become the custom to invite guest Italian ballerinas for important performances, but Kschessinskaya—so small, flirtatious, and feminine—had a tremendous will and surprising physical strength. She succeeded in making the Italians superfluous.

KSCHESSINSKAYA

She appeared to symbolize the last days of Imperial Russia. Lenin thought so, anyway, when he made a point of using the balcony of her last St. Petersburg home—a small palace built and decorated entirely to her taste—for his famous speech when he reached Russia in 1917. She had already fled with her Grand Duke André and their son, leaving everything except the jewels they were able to take with them. When these were all sold she opened a school in Paris and for three or four summers in the thirties I was among the pupils to whom she tried to impart some of her magic. It was marvellous to see that vivacity—the sparkling eyes, the fresh charm of a woman who would never lose the vestiges of fairy tale clinging around her. She died shortly before her one-hundredth birthday.

Kschessinskaya's contemporary and, in some ways her rival, was the adorable Olga Preobrajenskaya. They were as different as chalk from cheese. Preobrajenskaya—called Preo for short—was never very rich, never spoiled, not very pretty, but she was witty and industrious. She had a sort of pixie humour, sometimes suddenly angry, then in a few minutes smiling again. At the Maryinsky they cast her in roles like the White Cat in *The Sleeping Beauty*, roles which suited her personality and which she turned into a triumph; but by sheer hard work she also made herself into a great ballerina. She too taught in exile, in Paris, until only a couple of years before her death in 1962, when she was a mere ninety-two. She was the most respected teacher of her time, and I was lucky enough to have the benefit of her wise instruction whenever I was in Paris.

These great Imperial ballerinas had themselves been inspired as students by the Italian Virginia Zucchi, who went to St. Petersburg in 1885 at a time when, Petipa notwithstanding, the Maryinsky audience was apathetic to ballet. Zucchi danced first at a summer theatre in some pleasure gardens, causing such a furor with her intense dramatic acting, and a solo danced entirely on her pointes, that all St. Petersburg rushed to see her. When the Imperial Theatre re-opened for the winter season she was offered an engagement, which resulted in continuing visits over seven years and a strong revival of enthusiastic public attendance at the ballet. Petipa was surprised and impressed by her passionate interpretation of his works. Passion had no great part in his ballets; it was the meticulous construction of his scenarios and choreography that made them so great and so lasting. Sadly, these qualities lost their appeal for the young generation by the end of his life, and he died in bitterness, never suspecting that they would one day be revived. The root of his bitterness could also have been that, in spite of his considerable renown and his many very great successes, he never received a call to present even one work at the Paris Opera, where

AS THE WHITE CAT IN *THE SLEEPING BEAUTY*   WITH PIERINA LEGNANI IN *LE CORSAIRE*

IN *BLUEBEARD*   IN *MATADOR*

his brother was principal dancer and sometime ballet master. This would have been the crowning glory for Petipa, a Frenchman, but he waited for it in vain all his life.

Unwittingly, I suppose, Petipa was the cause of a Russian colleague suffering a similar fate. Since nineteenth-century life moved at a slower pace than ours, less importance was given to change or innovation, and theatre directors considered that one good ballet master at a time was sufficient to carry on the tradition. Petipa had waited so long to inherit his position from Saint-Léon that he was over seventy by the time he came to create *The Sleeping Beauty.* Five years later, because of ill-health, he handed over part of the choreography of *Swan Lake* to his assistant Lev Ivanov, who made of the second act the ultimate masterpiece of classical ballet. Logically, he should have succeeded to Petipa's position as principal ballet master instead of remaining always under his supervision.

Ivanov was more emotional than Petipa. The Frenchman was patient, diligent, and thorough; the Russian was sensitive, poetic, and fatalistic. In his youth he must have been the most engaging person—gifted, generous, carefree, intelligent. He could play by ear any piece of music he had heard only once, and his memory for ballets was equally prodigious.

VIRGINIA ZUCCHI IN *LA ESMERALDA*   LEV IVANOV

UNIFORMS FOR THE IMPERIAL BALLET SCHOOL, ST. PETERSBURG

CLASS AT THE IMPERIAL BALLET SCHOOL (TAMARA KARSAVINA: FRONT ROW, FOURTH FROM THE RIGHT)

IMPERIAL THEATRE SCHOOL STUDENTS, 1893-94
(PAVLOVA: SECOND KNEELING GIRL ON LEFT)

But, poor man, he had reached his half-century before he was appointed Petipa's assistant and there he was stuck—he died while the industrious Frenchman was still in command. I do not think it too fanciful to suggest that had Ivanov been able to pursue his own inspiration freely it would have brought him to something very similar to *The Fountain of Bakhchisarai* produced in Leningrad in 1934. Soviet ballet grows directly out of the Petipa-Ivanov heritage, but if Ivanov had been able to take over from Petipa, the evolution would have been smoother and quicker. In the event, an incredible generation gap arose. Ivanov died in 1901, two years before Petipa created his last ballet, and the next choreographer to emerge was sixty-two years younger than the great master!

MICHAEL FOKINE

FOKINE

As a result, the new choreographer, Michael Fokine, could not appreciate the solid virtues of Petipa's work; he found the old ballets stilted and artificial, nothing more than vehicles with which to exploit virtuosity. He saw that ballerinas wore tutus and toe shoes whether they were supposed to be princesses or goldfish; that a pas de deux of love was performed by two people who never even glanced at each other, only at the public; and that conversations between the characters were conveyed in arbitrary mime gestures as rigid as semaphore. Conversely, his own ideas were not well received by the old guard of the Maryinsky, although some of the younger dancers supported him. A small group that included Pavlova and Karsavina gathered round him to plot a revolt against the director, but it came to nothing.

FOKINE AND KARSAVINA IN *FISHERMAN AND THE PEARL FROM SHAVOTTA*

I imagine Fokine's ideal life would have been as successor to Petipa, breaking—as Ivanov had failed to do—the long line of Frenchmen who had held the position of choreographer in his theatre. Had he remained in Russia that might have happened. Instead, when the Revolution came he was already an international figure belonging as much to Paris, which had seen his greatest triumphs, as to his own country; so he became an exile, and as such started the reverse migration from Russia to the West. It was really Diaghilev's doing, for he was the one who pulled the strings that first took Fokine out of Russia.

Serge Diaghilev came of a moderately wealthy family in Perm, in the Urals, and it wasn't until he finished his schooling there that he went to St. Petersburg in 1890. He was ex-

PAVLOVA AND FOKINE IN *HARLEQUINADE*

tremely intelligent with an unusual aesthetic sensibility and forceful assurance behind a deceptively soft façade. The "Pickwickians," a group of young men who met regularly to discuss art and ideas, admitted him to their circle. They were high-spirited, full of energy, enthusiasm, wit, and irony, and they cared deeply about art and life.

One of them described Diaghilev at the time as "thick-set, plump, fresh-complexioned and a typical sturdy provincial." He was also shy, but he soon dominated them all in spite of the fact that he was neither writer, painter, nor musician himself. When he said, "I am first a charlatan, though rather a brilliant one; secondly a great charmer; thirdly frightened of nobody; fourthly a man with plenty of logic and very few scruples; fifthly, I seem to have no real talent," he forgot to say that he was a born leader, organizer, and *showman,* in

SERGE DIAGHILEV

the most complimentary sense of the word. For a short time, from 1899 to 1901, the Maryinsky Theatre, in a genuine effort to catch up with the times, engaged him as an artistic consultant. But there was never any possibility that he could have worked within a cumbersome bureaucracy. He was arrogant, uncompromising, and right.

Diaghilev did not set out to revolutionize ballet; it was almost forced on him by circumstances. In 1906 the Pickwickians presented an important exhibition of Russian art, and Diaghilev, by now very cosmopolitan, decided to show it in Paris—which was the cultural centre of the world but knew nothing of Russian painting. Encouraged by this success, he decided the next summer to introduce Russian music—also practically unknown to the capital of civilization—and gave a season of concerts with the great Chaliapin.

Obviously Diaghilev had the heart and courage of a gambler—he loved the excitement and risk of being an impressario of the arts, and Paris was his natural element. In 1908 he expanded to Russian opera, with *Boris Godunov*. Yet still he hadn't thought about the ballet; although Paris led the world in music and art, the state of ballet was abysmal. The person who suggested taking the Russian ballet to Paris in 1909 was Alexandre Benois, one of the founder Pickwickians.

Benois, a painter, had loved the ballet since childhood—a passion denied to Diaghilev in the provinces—and he had already planned a new ballet that had been produced in St. Petersburg two years before. The Pickwickians, who planned everything together, decided that this ballet, called *Le Pavillon d'Armide*, would be an excellent choice to introduce the exciting young dancers of the Maryinsky Theatre to Paris. Because that season—with Pavlova, Karsavina, and Nijinsky—was such a resounding success, the ballet was presented alone in 1910. Only then did Diaghilev and his friends begin to create bal-

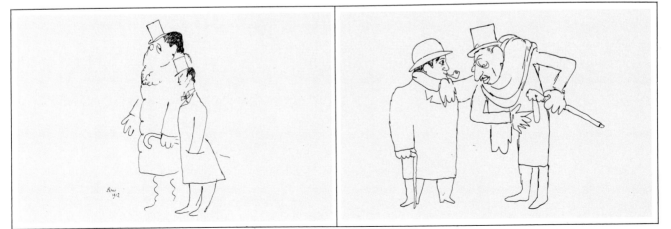

CARICATURES BY COCTEAU: DIAGHILEV AND NIJINSKY; PICASSO AND STRAVINSKY

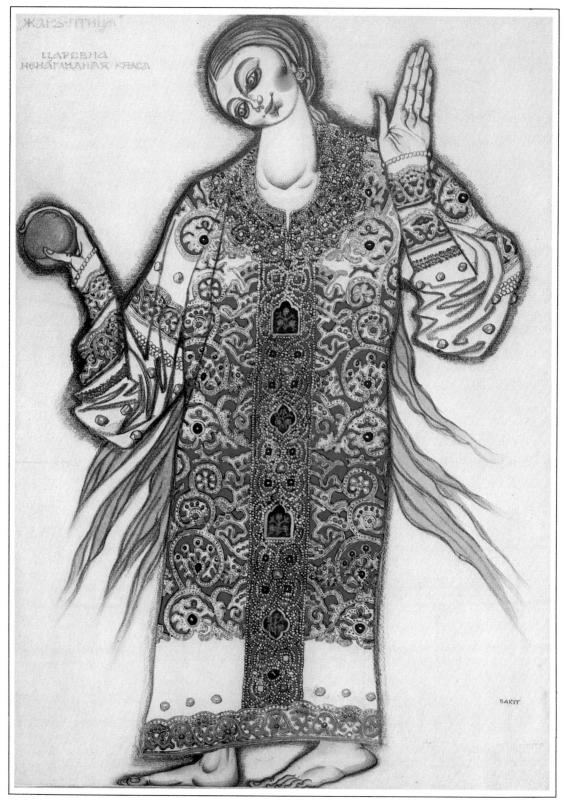

THE PRINCESS, *THE FIREBIRD*, BY LÉON BAKST

THE FIREBIRD (DESIGNED FOR KARSAVINA), BY BAKST

SYLVESTRA, *THE GOOD-HUMORED LADIES* DANSE SACRÉ

CONFIDANTE OF KOSTCHEI, *THE FIREBIRD* LITTLE AMERICAN GIRL, *LA BOUTIQUE FANTASQUE*

PERSIAN WOMAN, *THE FIREBIRD*

LE PELERIN, *LE DIEU BLEU*

LE MARÉCHAL, *THE SLEEPING PRINCESS*

NYMPHE, *L'APRÈS-MIDI D'UN FAUNE*

THE FAIRGROUND SCENE, *PETROUCHKA*, BY ALEXANDRE BENOIS

LA BOUTIQUE FANTASQUE, BY BAKST

SCENE I, *THE SLEEPING PRINCESS*, BY BAKST

THE GOOD-HUMOURED LADIES, BY BAKST

PAVLOVA, BY COCTEAU

lets expressly for Paris, making use of Léon Bakst's incredible imagination for theatre delight. His *Cléopâtre* had fascinated the French the previous year, so a new work was planned called *Schéhérazade,* barbaric and exotic with music by Rimsky-Korsakov and costumes that only Bakst could have dreamed up.

 Schéhérazade struck Paris like a thunderbolt and threw the Parisians into a decorative orgy of their own; couturier designers went oriental, and no chic home failed to have exotic cushions and decorations à la Ballet Russe. Also in that same short summer season Igor Stravinsky's first ballet, *The Firebird,* was produced. It was another mixture of fantasy and colour but most remarkable for Stravinsky's music. He was still very young—a tiny

KARSAVINA, BY COCTEAU

bird-like man—unknown outside Russia and little known even there, so it was a bold decision to give him a major ballet for Paris.

The season of 1910 was a limited summer engagement using dancers contracted to the Imperial Theatres. Only in 1911 did Diaghilev form a permanent company for which he had to find year-round employment and private patronage.

From that moment he was in a trap of his own making. The initial impact of Russian art on Paris had been sensational; in the following years it would be increasingly difficult to match it.

From the start he was totally dependent on his collaborators, even while he ruled

NIJINSKY AND PAVLOVA IN *LE PAVILLON D'ARMIDE*

TAMARA KARSAVINA

them despotically. They included Benois, who designed many of the settings; Bakst, whose extravagant designs and colour mixtures are still as original and exciting as they were in 1910; and Fokine, the choreographic reformer, and many others, especially painters and musicians, who were essential to Diaghilev at various times.

The one artist who needed him least was his ballerina, Tamara Karsavina. With or without Diaghilev, in Paris or in St. Petersburg, she was the most beautiful, most intelligent, and most perfect product of the Maryinsky Theatre. She was not a spirit of dance, she was a woman of rare calibre, intellectually a match for Diaghilev with her exceptional knowledge, taste, and judgement; and, as a ballerina, the master of both Petipa's disciplined classicism and Fokine's modern expressionism.

Fokine needed Karsavina to interpret his ballets and she cherished the experience of his contemporary works; in this respect she and Fokine were an ideal combination. No one could have danced his ballets more sensitively than did Karsavina; no one could have given her more magical roles than did Fokine. Under the guidance of Diaghilev he produced *Les Sylphides, Petrouchka, The Firebird, Le Spectre de la Rose*—the masterpieces of

KARSAVINA AND ADOLPH BOLM IN *THE FIREBIRD*

the period 1909 to 1911. Their special quality lies in their greater dependence on mood and atmosphere than on choreographic exactitude, and they are very difficult to reproduce satisfactorily because they require that every artist on the stage become the creature of Fokine's imagination. Karsavina was able to do this and add some magic of her own. And of course this was true of the other dancer essential to Diaghilev's success—Vaslav Nijinsky.

Diaghilev was a man of deep emotions, but his emotional loves were inextricably bound up with his artistic ones. He was always half in love with the artistry and beauty of Karsavina, and by no chance could he have felt passion for a handsome but stupid person—man or woman. By 1910 he had fallen in love with the genius of Nijinsky as an artist and, consequently, with Nijinsky himself. Undoubtedly the twenty-year-old dancer was unique. Karsavina in her autobiography, *Theatre Street,* describes the impression he made when she saw him for the first time. By chance she had arrived early in the studio where the senior students were finishing class:

> *I glanced casually, and could not believe my eyes; one boy in a leap rose far above the heads of the others and seemed to tarry in the air. "Who is this?" I asked Michael Oboukoff, his master. "It is Nijinsky; the little devil never comes down with the*

music." He then called Nijinsky forward by himself and made him show me some steps. A prodigy was before my eyes. He stopped dancing, and I felt it was all unreal and could not have been; the boy looked quite unconscious of his achievement, prosy and even backward. "Shut your mouth" were his master's parting words, "you fly-swallower." The ninth wonder of the world ran off down the corridor with the other boys.

Elsewhere in her book, Karsavina says that during their first performance in Paris, Nijinsky, on the spur of the moment, substituted a leap instead of a run to make his exit. He rose into the air from somewhere in mid-stage and sailed out of sight into the wings without losing height, leaving the public incredulous and spellbound. His gift of flight was part of his magic, but more important was his identification with each role he danced. Without the ballets Diaghilev caused Fokine to create for Nijinsky, he would still have been a matchless dancer, but less legendary, because the existing classical repertoire of

VASLAV NIJINSKY

WITH KARSAVINA IN *LE SPECTRE DE LA ROSE*

IN *L'APRÈS-MIDI D'UN FAUNE*

IN *SCHÉHÉRAZADE*

IN *LE ROI CANDAULE*

noble princes and characterless virtuosi did not suit him; they did not exploit his unique qualities. He was at the greatest disadvantage, in fact, in those roles of flesh-and-blood young men, yet it was not for lack of manly strength; as the Golden Slave in *Schéhérazade* his power was superhuman. At a loss to define his genius, various people used comparisons like "half-cat," "half-snake," "a panther," "a serpent," "a stallion," "no man, but a devil." It is a curious fact that he was rarely compared to a human being.

The circumstances of Diaghilev's decision to form his own permanent company must certainly have been closely related to his feelings for Nijinsky, and, as he loved intriguing, some people believe he purposely precipitated an incident at the Maryinsky Theatre so that Nijinsky would be released from his binding obligation to dance there. The incident involved the decency, or otherwise, of a costume he wore for *Giselle* at a performance attended by the Dowager Empress and her grandchildren, the Czar's daughters.

Some say the Dowager Empress was shocked because Nijinsky did not wear the customary little shorts under his close-fitting jacket—and the jacket was unusually short anyway over his tights, worn as all male dancers wear them today. The Dowager Empress explained afterward to a friend that even if she had noticed any indecency, it would not have been etiquette for her to admit it. The theatre director, however, did apparently think the costume unacceptable, and he was terribly embarrassed that members of the imperial family were in the audience. So the next morning he fired Nijinsky. Diaghilev now had Nijinsky as part of his personel and professional life, and he knew he could make the best ballet company in the world.

Only Diaghilev would have dreamed of making a choreographer out of Nijinsky, least of all a choreographer to replace Fokine; that was the Diaghilev flair, his extraordinary instinct for possibilities that others would never believe could exist. Yet Nijinsky had very clear and original ideas of his own. He was probably one of the greatest innovators of the century. Unfortunately, of the four ballets he created, only *L'Après-Midi d'un Faune* is preserved; the choreography of the others is unrecorded, so we can only imagine their effect.

The legend that comes down to us is of Nijinsky the phenomenal dancer, who, after a brief career of ten years, went mad. The drama of his relationship with Diaghilev is woven into the legend. It was a perfect artistic union but an imperfect love affair. Nijinsky, with his primitively powerful involvement in dance, was detached from the humdrum chores of ordinary life; Diaghilev, by contrast, was a man of extreme sophistication and sensibility, utterly civilized. They were both rare people, worthy of each other and complementing each other as artist and art lover, and on that level Nijinsky, in his curious otherwordly innocence, believed their union immune against every interference, including his own marriage—made in 1913 to a beautiful Hungarian girl he hardly knew—without even the courtesy of forewarning his benefactor and protector. He was amazed—more than that, incredulous—at Diaghilev's reaction to the news. It came via the company manager in the form of a curt telegram of dismissal.

On an instant Nijinsky was out of work; and so individual were the ballets Diaghilev had built around him that there was not another company in the world that could accommodate him. He could not return to the conventional star roles of the Maryinsky Theatre, which didn't suit him, and as for the other opera houses of Europe, their ballets were so antiquated as to make it impossible to include him without a complete re-organization of repertoire. When Nijinsky put together a group of dancers for a London theatre, he found they had to share the program with common variety acts. He was deeply upset. Nowhere did there exist the artistic background he needed.

How unimaginable that situation would be today: Nijinsky out of work! Now there are ballet companies north, east, south, and west that could present him most fittingly were he suddenly to soar in through an open window like the Spirit of the Rose.

Perhaps Nijinsky's most modern or timeless quality was his androgynous ambiguity of movement—the softness of his strength that some people saw as femininity, but I think was more the pliancy of a tiger, or of the King of Beasts. That family known as "the larger cats" are not feminine—they are powerful and stealthy, they tread silently, they spring with incredible coordination with every inch of their bodies, they seem suspended in the air before they land with such melting softness. A tiger in the jungle is totally integrated with his surroundings—instinctively dependent on, and involved in, every sound and movement, intensely concentrated and aware. That is how I imagine Nijinsky onstage. Diaghilev gave him his jungle. When he took it back, Nijinsky was lost, disoriented like an animal caught in an unfriendly cage. His cage consisted of the realities and responsibilities of life: a family to support on no income, business letters to write, war-time frontiers, visas, in-laws—a nightmare without dance, which to him was synonymous with life. His mind chose to leave his body and went, perhaps, to live alone in the deep green safety of a private, inaccessible jungle; his body remained, bereft, for thirty years.

The pattern of Diaghilev's life, without Nijinsky, continued as before, but perhaps

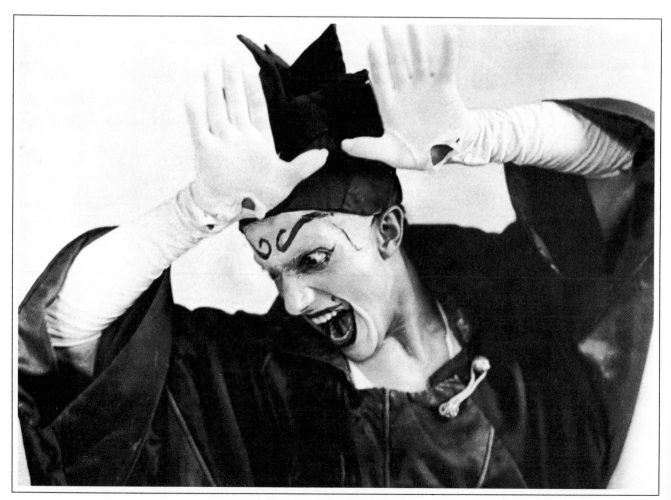

LÉONIDE MASSINE IN *PARADE*

never with the same spark. He discovered new choreographers, among them Nijinsky's sister, Bronislava Nijinska, Léonide Massine, and George Balanchine. He sought out new composers and painters who might never otherwise have been involved with ballet at all—Picasso was one. It was Diaghilev's genius that brought ballet, with one giant step, into the twentieth century.

It is incredible to think that he was able to keep it going single-handed, with no secure financing, for twenty years, including the period of the First World War, and until his death in 1929. He died young, in his middle fifties, and, at that moment, his Ballets Russes ended abruptly. His influence continued; his choreographers continued their work the better for having started under his guidance. George Balanchine was the last to be launched and has achieved the most.

Balanchine is a Georgian, he has his own mind, one might say his own cussedness, and his style is more classical than any of Diaghilev's other choreographers, but with his own modern twist.

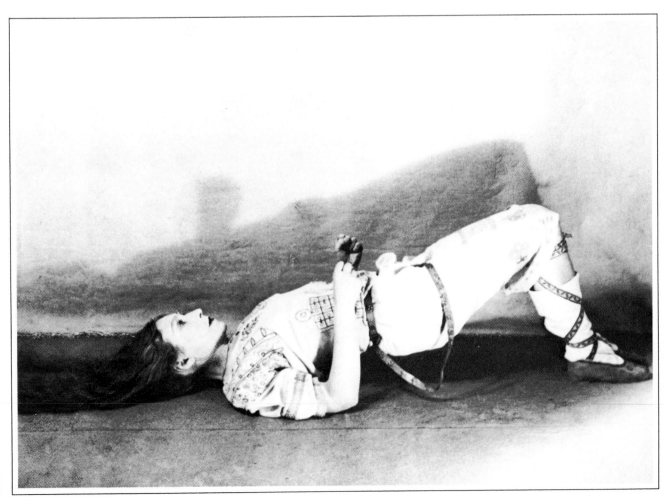

LYDIA SOKOLOVA IN MASSINE'S *THE RITE OF SPRING*

SERGE LIFAR AND ALEXANDRA DANILOVA IN THE ORIGINAL PRODUCTION OF BALANCHINE'S *APOLLON MUSAGÈTE*

GEORGE BALANCHINE, VENICE, MID-1920'S

Balanchine was a student in the Leningrad school throughout the war and Revolution, and choreographed his first ballets in Russia. Only in 1924, touring Germany with a group of Soviet State dancers, did he meet Diaghilev and subsequently join the Russians in exile. Thus he completed—with Fokine, Nijinsky, and Massine—the quartet of choreographers who came to the West in exchange, as it were, for the four Frenchmen—Didelot, Perrot, Saint-Léon, and Petipa—who had given so much to Russia. Curiously enough, they can be paired off fairly neatly. Didelot and Fokine liked their ballets to look convincingly realistic even if they were supernatural; Perrot and Nijinsky were the two best dancers and most modern choreographers of their time; Saint-Léon and Massine were masters of light comedy; and there are quite a few satisfying parallels between the lives of Petipa, who put his seal on Russian ballet, and Balanchine, who created American classicism. They made their first choreographies at eighteen and twenty respectively; were about thirty when they moved to their adopted countries, Russia and America; and were forty-four when they reached the culminating position of their careers, directing, one the Maryinsky Ballet, and the other the New York City Ballet. Each has been associated closely with a composer of particular importance to ballet, Tchaikovsky and Stravinsky. Balanchine has said, "Dance is woman," and there speaks his St. Petersburg schooling and outlook. Petipa also exalted the ballerina.

Superficially, Balanchine choreography doesn't resemble Petipa's. For one thing, Balanchine seems more concerned with patterns moving on the ground than with the composition of pictures. He will end a ballet with the dancers in a uniform pose, all kneeling, whereas Petipa might have arranged them in a design of varying heights. That is an aspect of Balanchine's uncluttered lines and patterns. His female dancers have the elongated, curveless figure that is so different from the nineteenth-century ideal. Balanchine uses a broad sweep of movement and long line, his arabesques are startlingly high; Petipa used small twinkling steps or sustained movements for his shorter, rounder dancers. Yet the technique is basically the same, the difference being what is accentuated and what is played down.

Neither master wanted to be too closely involved in expressing strong emotions. Each created his form of pure dance hinting at relationships without underlining them. Petipa was obliged to think in terms of a scenario divided into scenes of action and scenes of dance, with several main characters involved in a plot that used contrasting types of dance, and so on. It could very well be that, like Balanchine, he would have preferred to show dance for its own sake without the element of drama. The proof of this would seem to be in *La Bayadère,* as we see it now in the West—one scene from a complicated four-act tragedy, first produced in 1877, and a pure masterpiece of abstract ballet.

It is difficult to appreciate what is new without knowing what went before, so it is possible that only when the British ballet showed *The Sleeping Beauty* and *Swan Lake* in New York in 1949 did the American public acquire a dimension against which to measure Balanchine's originality. The old Petipa-Ivanov ballets, in all their magnificence, put into relief the American streamlined classic dancer in her unadorned costume pared down to enhance her line and movement. She is Balanchine's version of Petipa's standard tutu-clad

ballerina who is currently on the way to becoming a vanished species. There are very few important new ballets based on this nineteenth-century conventional ballet uniform. It is rather a sad thought that one day soon the tutu will be a dodo.

The parallel with Balanchine ends here. Petipa, at the end of his life, impeded the progress of ballet because he was a monopoly. He worked in a vacuum, out of touch with other ideas, both he and his St. Petersburg public undisturbed and settled in their ways. There is no such danger in New York, where every voice speaks out. No public has ever had such a choice of dance arrayed before it. There are opportunities to see the old, the new, the dramatic, the abstract, and the far-out experimental. What one company lacks can be found in another. This means that dance is in fine fettle—it has never been better. After St. Petersburg 1890 and Paris 1909, one can add a new peak: New York today.

SYMPHONY IN THREE MOVEMENTS

DANCE AERIAL

Stockholm, in the clear northern light, was a city of around 75,000 people in the year 1800—a flourishing European capital with that special atmosphere of a seaport, where ships moor up in the middle of town and there is a salt tang in the air. It was quite cosmopolitan and had a well-ordered ballet company founded in 1773 under King Gustaf III, following the French fashion adopted a little earlier in St. Petersburg.

The ballet had good relations with the Paris Opera, from where in 1803 there came a young Italian named Filippo Taglioni, engaged as a principal dancer. He was twenty-five years old, and I imagine him as a very personable young man, not the greatest dancer in the world, but intelligent, disciplined, and ambitious. He was to become the cornerstone of quite a little dynasty; already there were three other dancers in the family—his brother, his sister, and his father.

Filippo's Italian charm seems to have quickly overwhelmed Sophie Karston, the daughter of a famous Swedish singer; he didn't lose much time in marrying Sophie, nor in extending the dynasty. Their daughter Marie was born in Stockholm on April 23rd, 1804, within a year of the wedding. She and her father, between them, were to forge the image of the ballerina that we now take for granted, standing on one toe in an airy arabesque with full skirts floating out from her small waist, and a crown of flowers on her head. No such creature existed in 1804. Ladies in the ballet still wore some abbreviated version of the high-waisted Empire style that had come in after the French Revolution: a slim-cut dress of light material, with a bodice not much more than a modern bra. These costumes, worn to about calf length, allowed the dancers plenty of freedom to show their footwork and springy, bouncing elevation, and they adapted well to the attitudes and poses thought fit and proper at the time.

Ballet plots were either those surviving from pre-Revolutionary days and concerned exclusively with mythological and allegorical subjects, or they were stories of peasants and

FILIPPO TAGLIONI

the bourgeoisie. They romanticized the peasantry in the same way Marie Antoinette had done, playing stylishly at being a milkmaid in her rustic hamlet at Versailles.

The newer ballets were more robust and amusing than their staid allegorical fore-runners. Comic bumpkins and servants, Turks, Chinese, seafaring, farm, and townsfolk were now the lively heroes and heroines of literature, painting, and the theatre. Such stories also meant that scenic designers could forget the vague limbo inhabited by gods and goddesses and deal instead with houses, streets, gardens, and country settings, made breathtakingly realistic by their superb mastery of perspective.

Marie Taglioni made her début in 1822 in a ballet of the mythological type—*A Nymph Presented at the Court of Terpsichore*—which must have been a light-hearted affair, as one of the critics observed that she was a "demi-caractère dancer, inclining to the grace-ful rather than the serious, who could devote herself successfully to the comedy-mime style." That is far from what she became later—so much for critics! A Danish ballet, *The Whims of Cupid and the Ballet Master*, first performed in 1786 and preserved in the reper-toire of the Royal Theatre, Copenhagen, to the present, gives a good idea of the dancing style of the day. It mixes the mythological and peasant themes in a humorous ballet that includes a comical dance for two Quakers.

Filippo Taglioni was to change the face of ballet completely. Much has been written about his daughter, but I find him really much more interesting because it was he who made her success—and what a marvellously indomitable man he was! Quite amazing in his degree of dedication to his family and his work, and his life wasn't easy at all, although there were moments of great glory. He was born and brought up in Italy, dancing and travelling like his father and younger brother, and making his début in Pisa when he was seventeen. By the time he was twenty-two he was at the Paris Opera and from there he went to Stockholm. But he didn't stay long. After Marie was born, the new family moved on to Vienna and was increased by the birth of a son, Paul, when Marie was four years old.

Filippo was twenty-seven when Marie was born, fifty-five when he created *La Sylphide* for her, and sixty-nine when she retired from the stage. Still, he worked for another three years, then retired to Lake Como, where he died at the age of ninety-four. Marie outlived him by only thirteen years. Paul, his son, was also a successful dancer and choreographer (he produced the first ballet that used electric light—it was in London in 1849—and in another ballet he used roller-skates!), and Paul's daughter, Marie the Second, was a very good ballerina in the family tradition.

No one knows precisely when Filippo began to make a dancer of his daughter. We do know that when she was twelve he took her to the best professor in Paris, the aged Jean-François Coulon, with whom he himself had studied. Coulon took one look at her and said something to the effect of "What do you expect me to do with that little hunchback?" So began the career of one of the most auspicious names in the history of dance. I suppose that Filippo, coming of a dancing family, would have put his children to dance whatever they were like, so the fact that Marie was stoop-shouldered and skinny with over-long arms, not to mention that she was quite plain, did not make any difference. But it did make a difference to Marie, who was mocked by the other pupils and played truant whenever she could. No doubt, in the circumstances, she was not enthusiastic about the career chosen for her by her father, but there was nothing whatever that she or her mother could do about it. Father made the decisions, and that was that, and in any case he was still away in Vienna, where he held the position of dancer and ballet master.

Sophie was a soft-hearted mother; she sent very encouraging reports of Marie's progress, even though at the Opera she was told, "Make a dressmaker of your daughter, for she will never be a good dancer. I know your husband too well not to be sure that he would never want his child to be merely someone hanging about backstage." These were the words of ballet master Jean Aumer, when Marie was seventeen; but Filippo had mean-

THE MAZURKA OF *LA GITANA*

LA SYLPHIDE

LA GITANA

LA BAYADÈRE

MARIE TAGLIONI AND HER BROTHER, PAUL TAGLIONI, IN *LA SYLPHIDE*, 1834

while sent for his family and arranged a début for Marie in Vienna a few months later at his theatre, the Kärntnertor. She was to appear as the principal dancer in a ballet he would create for her—no question of working up through the corps de ballet in the usual way.

This is mere supposition, but I believe things must have gone something like this: Filippo, looking forward to being reunited with his family and seeing his daughter's progress, might have been tempted to drop a word or two like "She's studying with Coulon in Paris, you know" or "I hear she's getting on well" and so on. The day came when his wife and children arrived after days of bumping along in the post chaise from Paris. Filippo was anxious to see Marie's dancing and although she was a bit weak from the journey she did the best she could. He was appalled! He realized that she was nowhere near the standard he expected; he felt his own name and reputation were at stake in Vienna, perhaps his position too. Besides, he was Italian, and I don't think he would have liked the humiliation of cancelling the whole affair and putting her in the back row of the corps de ballet, which was the place she merited. There must have been a good deal of tension in the family that day, but Filippo was a man of character and he knew there was only one remedy for the drastic situation they were in, so he drew up a crash course and set to work.

For all that he adored Marie, I doubt that he gave a thought to her feelings. His program was put into operation immediately—six hours of work a day divided into three periods that fitted in with his duties at the theatre and allowed Marie time to rest and recover. She has left a description of those days in some detail: two hours in the morning, exercising tendons and muscles to strengthen the legs and feet; two hours in the middle of the day devoted to equilibrium, called aplomb; two hours at night practising all kinds of jumping steps, "difficult, tiring, and dangerous." Normally, one session of two hours a day would be adequate. Frequently at the end of a lesson she would cry and collapse, exhausted. Sometimes she fainted. Her mother waited anxiously in the next room, ready with warm water and a sponge to refresh her and to give words of comfort as she changed her into dry clothes. Sophie was distressed by the severity of her husband's treatment, but it was the only way Marie could be ready in time for the announced début.

At last the great day came, and when it was all over, Filippo, who had also danced in the ballet, took out his diary before going to bed and wrote: "10th June, 1822. For the first time that my daughter Marie appeared on the stage, she obtained the very greatest success." I can just see him putting down the pen and clasping his hands across his waistcoat in deep satisfaction. Marie was eighteen years old.

After all they had been through to reach that lowest rung of the ladder, the family

CARICATURE OF TAGLIONI
BY THÉOPHILE WAGSTAFF (PSEUDONYM FOR WILLIAM M. THACKERAY), 1836

was committed to Marie's career irrevocably. In the ensuing years, until he was able to arrange her first trial performances in Paris—the system in force at the Opera demanded six before a contract was granted—he was able to polish and mould her technique, and when she did finally appear, the effect of her dancing was a revelation. As recorded by Lady Blessington, it was something totally new, "graceful beyond all comparison, wonderful lightness and absence of all violent effort, or at least the appearance of it, and a modesty as new as it is delightful to witness." She adds that Marie received the applause with "decent dignity, very unlike the leering smiles" of the other dancers, and that she elevated dance far beyond the "licentious style generally adopted by the ladies of her profession."

Marie's initial success at the Opera thoroughly upset some of the other ballerinas, who resorted to making the stage slippery with soap for her second appearance; thanks to Filippo, she was so assured in her dancing that none of this bothered her. Throughout her career it was the same story of incredible lightness and ease, the child-like smile and modest demeanour. Could there not be a very simple explanation for the "new" dancing of Marie Taglioni? Could it not be because she was trained by her father—and what father does not wish to see his daughter pure and virtuous? He moulded her character and her dancing in conformity with his feelings for this plain daughter whom he loved so dearly. Auguste Vestris, the most famous teacher in Paris, encouraged "provocative smiles and attitudes verging on the indecent and shameless." Filippo said to his pupils, "Ladies, mar-

AUGUST BOURNONVILLE

ried and unmarried, should be able to see you dance without occasion to blush." His own daughter would never show any tinge of the vulgarity common to many of her colleagues.

Filippo had formed a dancer who was technically superior to all her contemporaries. Her tendency to stoop had been remedied by driving her relentlessly till she stood straight. As for her long arms—which everyone considered a defect—he had taught her to cross them at the wrist instead of joining the tips of her fingers, and the positions he devised for her have remained in the choreography of certain ballets ever since, looking incongruous on short-armed dancers!

She had another drawback—her rather unemotional nature—and it was here that Filippo showed his brilliance when he created the character of the Sylphide for her. The immortal spirit, symbol of man's unattainable dreams, was so perfect for her ethereal dancing, her innocent, modest nature, and her cool temperament that her image comes down to us today as clearly as if she still lived. An elderly ballet critic in Paris when I was young was so fervent in his description of her dancing, as we sat together over a cup of tea, that he almost fell off his chair trying to demonstrate her flight. When I ventured to suggest that it was difficult for anyone to know exactly how she danced, as she had died half a century before, he looked at me and said flatly, "Of course I know, I have lived intimately with Mlle. Taglioni for the last fifteen years." Such was her spell.

La Sylphide epitomized the Romantic era in the arts. It is set in the mists of Scotland, where the kilted hero pursues a chaste vision none but he can see. He jilts his fiancée only to discover, with the help of some witches and their magic brew of snakes and frogs, that the immortal Sylphide cannot be grasped; his imaginary ideal does not exist, and in trying to possess it he destroys both the vision and himself. The whole thing seems rather naïve to our minds; but in a way it parallels the science fiction that is the romanticism of our time—the modern expression of man's eternal obsession with the unknown that *La Sylphide* expressed so aptly in 1832. It was not then a quaint, nostalgic piece of theatre but an immediate, modern experience.

Through a fortuitous happenstance of ballet history we can still see a Sylphide flying up the chimney, or vanishing from under a tartan rug thrown over her to conceal her presence in a chair, exactly as she did in the original performances. In the Royal Theatre in Copenhagen, the technique and style of the 1830's, with all their freshness and charm, were preserved absolutely intact for over one hundred years, part of the legacy of a remarkable dancer and ballet master, August Bournonville, who was just one year younger than Marie Taglioni. Bournonville staged his own version of *La Sylphide*—with new music by a Danish composer—just four years after it was first presented in Paris, and it is this version that gives us now as clear an impression of the original as it is possible to re-create after so long a time.

Bournonville was the son of a French ballet master, Antoine Bournonville, who—like Filippo—worked in Stockholm for a while, moving from there to Copenhagen, where August was born in August 1805. The boy was extremely talented and later studied in Paris, where he did so well that he became Marie Taglioni's favourite partner, but he decided his place was in Copenhagen, which he considered his home. From then on he dedicated his life to the Danish ballet and, being exceptionally intelligent as well as cultivated and of high moral integrity, he was able to raise his profession to a position of social respectability that it was denied in much of Europe. As a dancer he was a fine technician, so he gave himself—and his successors—quite as many opportunities to dazzle the audience as he gave his ballerinas. If he and his partner did the same step to opposite sides, he generally took the easier side for himself. This had been the natural order of things, and Bournonville preserved it that way in Copenhagen, whereas elsewhere, as the development of toe shoes opened up new choreographic possibilities for the ballerina, more help was needed from the poor male dancer who was so busy holding, catching, and spinning, then lifting, carrying, and eventually throwing her about that he was left very little time or energy for his own exhibitions of virtuosity. One could say that Bournonville preserved male dancing in Copenhagen by doing little to encourage the female use of toe shoes, and that Filippo destroyed male dancing in Paris by establishing the image of the ballerina as dancing essentially on her toes. But then Bournonville was himself a good dancer, whereas Filippo projected his ambitions onto his daughter and choreographed to show her off.

It is often said that Marie was the first to dance on her toes—it is one of the things for which she is famous. In fact, several ballerinas had begun to develop this technique before her, and while still in Vienna she and her father had watched Amalia Brugnoli, who astonished the public by standing on her toes, but all too obviously helped to raise herself up by taking the strain in her arms. This was a very understandable fault in view of the absence of adequate support in her shoes, which were a far cry from the blocked toes used today. Unquestionably, Filippo realized the possibilities of the new technique and understood what special strength was required to make it artistically valid. He thought up exercises for the foot and leg muscles so that the whole weight of the body could be supported gracefully on the toes of one foot. The shoe played very little part in it, as we can see by studying a pair actually worn by Marie. They are completely soft. Other dancers were praised for their cleverness in getting up onto their toes, but Marie was able to give the impression of coming down from the air to rest delicately for a moment before flying off again. That magic was hers alone.

It seems to me that Filippo is never given enough credit for the revolution he wrought in the art of ballet with *La Sylphide*. It was quite as innovative as the Diaghilev ballet in 1909, but Filippo achieved his revolution single-handedly; he had no home theatre like the Maryinsky in St. Petersburg to give him a traditional training, no Diaghilev, Benois, or Stravinsky to help him. He did everything himself—dancing, teaching, choreographing, designing costumes if necessary, taking charge of the music, arranging contracts and travel, and seeing to a hundred other details (all methodically noted in his diary, together with a list of the jewellery presented to Marie and guarded by him personally on their journeys). He was a marvellous father until he became senile in his last years and lost Marie's fortune in some foolish speculation. Even so, I believe he kept her love and respect to the end. He had stood by her like a rock through the many trials of fate that she had to weigh in the balance against her triumphs.

Marie had the misfortune to fall in love with and marry an attractive but worthless aristocrat, Count Alfred Gilbert de Voisins, who quickly became bored with the novelty of having the theatre's greatest celebrity as his wife. At about the same time that she lost him, her supremacy as a star was seriously challenged by a younger rival, Fanny Elssler. A little

MARIE TAGLIONI, *LEFT,* AND FANNY ELSSLER, *RIGHT,* YOUNG AND OLD

ELSSLER WITH HER SISTER THERESE, AND AT THE TIME OF HER DEBUT

later Marie again fell in love, this time with an altogether charming and worthy young man who died suddenly, of what is thought to have been meningitis, just at the moment when they were in Russia enjoying the most fantastic successes of her career. It is not surprising that she cited as her outstanding characteristic "resignation in adversity." At the end of her life, after her father had lost their savings, she found herself obliged to open a dancing school and chose London as the most suitable or agreeable site, perhaps because Paris held too many bitter memories among the triumphs. It was in London that she had said farewell to the stage, knowing she was always loved and respected there. Perhaps her favourite foods, listed on a questionnaire as bread and "le plum pudding," had clinched her choice!

From her many letters to close friends, one gathers that Marie was cheerful by nature and fond of a good gossip, especially at the expense of her colleagues, whom she did not praise readily—but why should she? Her father had set her very high standards, which few could match. To Emma Livry, the one dancer who might have reached those heights had she lived long enough, Marie was as generous and encouraging as a proud mother.

Two little pointers to theatrical customs of her time come out in Marie's letters. First, she talks just as much and as knowledgeably of prima donnas as of ballerinas, because ballet and opera performances were always integrated; even a long ballet shared the program with a complete opera. Second, she constantly refers to how much money one or another ballerina would bring into the theatre, not what fee she would get. This was because "benefits" were written into every artist's contract for each season, and on those benefit evenings the artist cleared all, or a large proportion of, the receipts, which varied according to the crowd they could draw and the ticket prices they could ask. They often sold the tickets personally from their lodgings. Filippo and Marie always kept an eye on the box office and knew down to the last franc or penny what every dancer was worth at a benefit.

No two dancers could have been more different than Taglioni and Fanny Elssler. Fanny introduced an artistic sex appeal that was in complete contrast to Marie's spiritual rule over Romantic ballet, and it was enough to put all Paris into a furore over which was the greater of the two. Half the city dropped Marie like a hot coal and became "Elsslerites" overnight; the other half remained loyal "Taglionistes," defending their idol.

The rivalry had been carefully plotted by the wily Dr. Véron, director of the Paris Opera, and the result far exceeded his hopes at the box office. Although he was originally a doctor of medicine, he had a real flair for the theatre, understood modern publicity techniques, and more or less invented the "star" system by giving Taglioni precedence over all his own French ballerinas at an unheard-of salary. When she had been supreme for five years he thought a rival was needed to give the public a fillip, so he went to take a look at Fanny and Therese Elssler, the Austrian ballerinas making a great name in London. Fanny, he decided, was just what he needed and, in his flamboyant, buccaneering manner, he wined and dined the sisters and served expensive jewels with the dessert while unfolding the terms of a three-year contract. The Elsslers were modest and reserved, such methods alarmed them, but, eventually, Therese, who took charge of the business, agreed.

One of the differences between the two rival stars was that Marie's career was ruled by her father and Fanny's by her sister—until the day she quarrelled with Therese over the status of their respective lovers, who lived with them in their apartment. Therese had quite a talent for choreography, which she generously used to further Fanny's success. They often danced together and Therese, being unusually tall, dressed in male costume to partner Fanny when the occasion required.

At that time dancers were still discovering new steps and finding new ways to use toe shoes. Marie's steps were all bounding and light; her father said, "I have never yet *heard* my daughter dancing — if ever that should happen I would have no more to do with her." He was indignant because, after he had installed a sloping floor, like the stage, in his lodgings so that Marie could practise, the gentleman occupying the room below had sent a message that the great ballerina should on no account worry about the noise disturbing him. Filippo didn't appreciate the courtesy at all.

Fanny's steps were often noisy as she attacked the stage with her toes in sharp, quick footwork that fascinated the audience. This was a technique in use by some dancers, but it is hard to know how they did it in such flimsy toe shoes. According to a contemporay description, Fanny had "great vivacity, astonishing strength, precision coming out of apparent disorder, rich pointes, an abundance of well beaten entrechats, much suppleness, legs which raise above the level of the hips, and eyes and head movements which are particularly enticing."

In spite of all that, and the fact that she was six years younger than Marie and very attractive, she still had terrible qualms about the Paris début which was preceded by Dr. Véron's most blatant publicity campaign; she ran to the old teacher Auguste Vestris, who helped her tremendously. It was he who urged others to "provocative smiles and attitudes verging on the indecent and shameless." I do not think, however, that he would have attempted to corrupt Fanny's natural decency; what he would have liked was her combination of vitality and feminine charm. She said he gave her grace and expression, but her greatest source of fulfillment she found later in the rhythms of national folk dance.

Some Spanish dancers appearing in Paris gave her the idea of a solo, *La Cachucha,* which became associated with her as *La Sylphide* did with Marie. It is amusing to contrast descriptions of Fanny's dance by a famous ballet master and a famous critic. August Bournonville said the dance began quietly, "as though inviting the audience to share a little joke, but in the second part her whole face lit up with a passionate glow which radiated a halo of joy. This moment never lost its effect, and from then on the whole dance became a game in which she drove the public crazy with delight." The critic Théophile Gautier, with his usual ridiculous effusion, wrote: "How she twists! How she bends! What fire! What voluptuousness! What ardour! Her swooning arms flutter about her drooping head, her body curved back, her white shoulders almost brush the floor."

The long-term result of Dr. Véron's playing the two stars one against the other was to spin them right out of the Paris scene altogether. Taglioni, tired of petty sniping and endless comparisons favouring her rival, journeyed to St. Petersburg with her father, mother, little daughter by the departed worthless husband, worthy new young lover, little dog, and a mountain of baggage. There she triumphed gloriously for three years.

Fanny, more imaginative and adventurous by far, accepted an offer from America, although she admitted to having a "very indistinct notion of its whereabouts." As the time

ELSSLER IN *THE ARTIST'S DREAM*

drew near, she wrote: "I cannot look upon this strange intention as other than a mad freak that has seized my fancy." The "mad freak" stretched out into two years of sensational success and excitement. She was accompanied by her cousin, Katti Prinster, in place of Therese, who was terrified of the sea; her partner and ballet master, James Sylvain; her coachman; and a maid. The year was 1840. Leaving London for Bristol to embark on *The Great Western*, the first steamship to convey passengers across the Atlantic, they had the added thrill of hurtling through the countryside in a train for the first time in their lives. It took them some thirty miles, as far as Reading, the end of the line, and the rest of the journey was by carriage, taking another ten hours. The Atlantic crossing lasted over two weeks because they were delayed by a terrible storm. Then, one bright morning, they sailed past Staten Island and saw the charming tree-shaded promenade of Battery Park.

It seems incredible that barely a fortnight after her arrival, the local corps de ballet, consisting of eight couples supplemented by some actors for the character roles, had learned the ballets and Fanny had got back into training—for it had been impossible to practice on board ship—for the première.

ELSSLER IN *LA CACHUCHA*

CARICATURE OF *LA CACHUCHA*

In the meantime, expectations had been mounting day by day and reached such a pitch that poor Fanny was almost paralyzed with terror. When the curtain rose for her opening dance, such a shout of welcome burst from the audience "as stunned my senses, and made me involuntarily recoil." The whole house was standing, men waving hats and women their handkerchiefs. The uproar lasted several minutes. This reception before she had danced a step made her, if possible, more nervous than before. The first dance went only moderately well, but with that she worked off her nerves and when it came to her second number, she felt herself bursting with energy and excelled anything she had ever done. Then the audience felt they had seen the Fanny they were waiting for. There followed a storm of applause, hysterical enthusiasm, and shouting and stamping in the galleries. The night was an overwhelming triumph.

From then on it was like a royal progress. Congress adjourned whenever she danced in Washington (President Van Buren's son was her escort), the city of New Orleans came to a standstill for the whole two weeks of her season, she was knee-deep in flowers wherever she went, and admirers nightly drew her carriage from the theatre to her hotel.

She could not resist the added adventure of accepting an invitation to the Tacón Opera House in Havana—the voyage past the shores of southern Florida was fraught with danger from hostile Indians if the ship should go aground, and in a nightmare she thought grinning savages roasted and ate her. On their arrival in Cuba, Fanny was not really surprised that local recruits for the corps had only the poorest conception of what ballet was about, and the theatre manager, realizing that their deep suntans were out of character for a group of sylphs, made them wear yellow camisoles to cover their arms. In spite of these imperfections, and the fact that on the evening of her benefit Fanny herself had to sit at a table in front of the theatre to receive the donations of gold coins, then run backstage and prepare for the performance (patrons gave more money with that system), she loved Havana and returned the following year. She was just about to risk bandits and yellow fever to continue on to Mexico when news came from Vienna that her father was ill. She decided all good things must come to an end and made plans to return to Europe.

Everything about Fanny's life was different from that of her rival. Marie was always under her father's wing. She maintained her aura of respectability in spite of divorce and an illegitimate child, always signing letters with her married name, Comtesse Gilbert de Voisins, née Taglioni.

Fanny made no concessions. Although she had two children, she never married; she lived her life in her own way, owing nothing to anyone, and answerable to no one. She made some sacrifices to provide for needy relations and supported herself in unostentatious comfort when she retired. As a child in Vienna she had been used to poverty. Her father, who was copyist and valet to Haydn until the composer's death, seems never after that to have earned much money or done anything useful. He must have been musical, lovable, and weak. The family was large and extremely poor, so Fanny and her two sisters were sent to dancing school early, in the hope that they would soon contribute some income.

There is a strange tale which resulted in Fanny giving birth to a son two weeks before her seventeenth birthday. The three Elssler girls were engaged to dance in Naples, where the king's licentious brother picked out Fanny and chose to seduce her. Their mother, who was supposedly chaperoning them, was forced to consent—or to sell her, as Fanny said uncomplainingly in later life—because the prince threatened to use his power in Vienna to prevent any member of the family prospering. One can just imagine what Filippo Taglioni's reaction would have been in the same circumstances!

After that bad start it was not unnatural that Fanny should have become attached to another man also much older than herself because Friedrich von Gentz was the opposite of the Italian Prince of Salerno. Gentz was extremely cultivated, a statesman, and very much

FANNY ELSSLER AND THE BALTIMOREANS

ELSSLER'S CARRIAGE PULLED BY ADMIRERS

a gentleman, who treated Fanny with deep respect, caring for her like a father. All his life he had been a ladies' man, handsome and distinguished. Suddenly, in his sixties, he was bowled over by Fanny. For her part, Fanny was flattered that so great a man should be at her feet and she grew very fond of him—finally, of her own will, becoming his mistress. It was not a long affair, but it had a deep influence on her. After Gentz, she was never able to put up with the company of an unintelligent man. That was the main reason she didn't marry; none of the men who courted her lived up to Gentz, and neither did those she found physically attractive. She might have loved the Duke of Reichstadt, Napoleon's romantic son, nicknamed l'Aiglon, who died of consumption when he was twenty-one. He missed no opportunity to see her dance, he was fascinated by her, but they couldn't meet; Fanny's mother was so anxious not to lose the protection of Gentz that she never let Fanny out alone. In any case, guessing that she would fall in love if she met the young duke, Fanny would not have taken the risk. She knew it would wound Gentz too gravely, perhaps kill him.

The first young lover she had, who fathered her second child when she was twenty-three, was a dashing Austrian dancer. She does not appear to have loved him, and their dancing commitments soon parted them. To the end she guarded her independence, and when she died in 1884 she was publicly mourned by the whole of Vienna, while Taglioni's death the same year in Marseilles went almost unnoticed.

QUEEN VICTORIA AND PRINCE ALBERT WALTZING, C. 1840

To celebrate Fanny's home-coming after her American tour, Vienna had a medal struck in her honour. It was 1842, and the entire city was dancing to the music of Johann Strauss, of whom they were justly proud; he was famous all over Europe and had played his waltzes for Queen Victoria at her coronation festivities. What the Viennese did not yet know was that Johann's son and namesake would be even more famous than his father. The young man was sixteen and passionately keen on music; his father was equally keen for him to become a banker. He had to study music in secret.

Two years later, when his father saw the announcement for his first concert, he was furious. "What!" he said, "and playing his own compositions too? But he knows nothing about waltzes!" How wrong he was. The younger Strauss outshone even his father with the beauty and variety of his compositons.

VALSE BLEUE

There is nothing very significant or meaningful in a waltz, it makes no obvious contribution to society, yet it has a marvellous lilt for dancing—and Strauss made it important to the lives of many people. The waltz was not a sudden invention, it had existed for years, danced by peasants, before the upper classes sought it out, following a natural law that, whenever their own dances began to bore them, they adopted a country dance to start a new fashion.

Who would believe now that such a harmless, simple thing as the waltz could have been greeted with absolute horror and suspicion when it first appeared in drawing rooms in the eighteenth century? A teacher of ballroom dancing commented tartly in 1767: "I can imagine that mothers are fond of the waltz, but not that they permit their daughters to dance it." Fifty years later, concern for the welfare of daughters was still used as an excuse

AN EARLY WALTZ

by the anti-waltz campaigners. A contributor to the London *Times* in 1816, reporting that the Prince Regent had brought the waltz to court, was beside himself with indignation about the "voluptuous intertwining of the limbs, the close compressure of the bodies in their dance, so far removed from the modest reserve which has hitherto been considered distinctive of English females. So long as this obscene display was confined to prostitutes and adulteresses, we did not think it deserving of notice; but now it is attempted to be forced on the respectable classes of society by the evil example of their superiors, we feel it a duty to warn every parent against exposing his daughter to so fatal a contagion."

Well! However that may have been, when Queen Victoria set her seal of approval by waltzing with Prince Albert in 1837, there was nothing more to be said. And where, I wonder, would ballet be without the waltz?

As soon as waltzing was no longer shocking to their elders, young people wanted something else as different as possible, and the answer came along in the form of the polka. This zany rhythm had them all kicking up their heels, with coattails flying in all directions, in wild abandon. It originated in Czechoslovakia, a country dance, of course, and is said to have been taken to Paris by an itinerant ballet master. For a while the polka was seen only in popular dance halls, but suddenly the upper-crust dance teachers got hold of it and high society went cavorting and spinning about in paroxysms. The dance spread from country to country like wildfire. It was almost like the dance manias of the Middle Ages, when the madness carried people from city to city, dancing all the way.

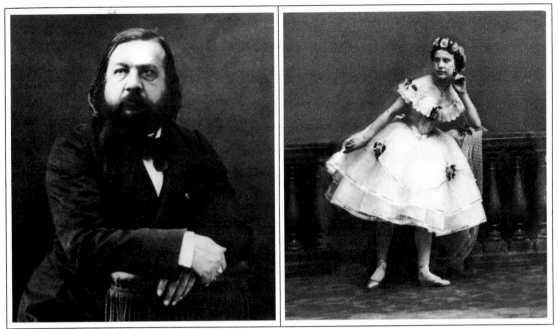

THÉOPHILE GAUTIER   FANNY CERRITO

The Bohemian polka was a natural for ballet. Carlotta Grisi was soon to be seen in London dancing it with her husband, Jules Perrot, at Her Majesty's Theatre, while Jean Coralli, ballet master at the Paris Opera, taught a version suitable for amateurs that was in conflict with the rules laid down by a famous society teacher named Cellarius. They got into such a terrible fight that their supporters arranged for a contest between the two masters. It was won by the ballet faction. Neither the Charleston, the twist, nor any of the other passing crazes affected people as violently as the 1840's polka.

It was just this period of the 1830's and 1840's that saw Romantic ballet, and its ballerinas, at their height. Taglioni and Elssler were the outstanding names among many more, all of them engaged at one time or another at the Paris Opera, and all of them subjects of Théophile Gautier's special brand of criticism. I would love to know what they thought as they read some of his reviews. "Let us begin with her physique, and then speak of her talent," sums up his attitude to each new dancer in turn. Fanny Cerrito was, according to Gautier, "short of stature and round in frame," and had "plump, dimpled arms . . . a delicate ankle and well-rounded leg. Her shoulders, her bosom do not have that scrawniness characteristic of female dancers whose whole weight seems to have descended into their legs." However, no one was perfect in his eyes: "Her waist cuts her body into two completely equal parts which is contrary to the laws of human proportions, and particularly unfavourable for a danseuse."

He described the Danish ballerina Lucile Grahn as "tall, slender, small-jointed and well-made, and would be prettier still if she did not wear such an obstinate smile"; while poor Adeline Plunkett, a Belgian ballerina, "is young, pretty, well-formed, with a dainty

FANNY CERRITO IN *LA SYLPHIDE*

CARLOTTA GRISI DANCING THE POLKA

LUCILE GRAHN IN *CATARINA OU LA FILLE DU BANDIT*

LOUISE FLEURY IN *THE BEAUTY OF GHENT*

foot, slender leg and charming features; but she is a little delicate for the stage and difficult to see in the distance."

Fanny Elssler was the one who drove him to the wildest excesses. In the course of various reviews we can gather: "She is tall, supple and well formed . . . satiny shoulders . . . slim wrists, delicate ankles . . . strong slender legs, very different from the ordinary dancer whose body seems to have shrunk into her stockings . . . the knee-caps are well-defined, stand out in relief and make the whole knee beyond reproach. . . ." Of course she had to have some imperfections too: "Her superb hair, lustrous and glossy, is not the right hair for the head or body . . . her eyes, very black, with their pupils like two little stars of jet set in a crystal sky, are inconsistent with her nose which like her forehead is German." (Another writer remembered her eyes when she was fourteen as "large and blue.") He explained that her smile, her white skin, and her placid brow were German but her hair, her tiny feet, her tapering hands, and the bold curve of her back were Spanish. "And this same indecision is to be seen in her sexual characteristics; her hips are rather undeveloped, her breasts no fuller than a hermaphrodite of antiquity." (He had previously said that "her

MEYERBEER'S *ROBERT LE DIABLE*, L'ACADÉMIE IMPÉRIALE DE MUSIQUE

GISELLE, ACT I

bosom is full, which is a rarity among dancers.") An English critic thought, "The exquisite management of her bust and arms—one of the most difficult things for a dancer—sets her apart from all others."

Later Gautier got carried away by the hermaphrodite comparison, saying, "Her arms, less rounded than a woman's, plumper than a girl's, suggest the form of a marvellously beautiful young man with a touch of effeminacy . . . the rest of her beauty is made still more attractive and piquant by this delicious ambiguity," and added the sly sentence, "This quality makes her pleasing even to those ladies who cannot stand the sight of a ballerina." He was always anxious to emphasize his admiration for the ladies and lack of it for male dancers—suspiciously so, one might think, especially as, when he did deign to mention Arthur Saint-Léon, he couldn't resist calling attention to his "hamstrings of steel."

Gautier was a poet and one of the leaders, with Victor Hugo, of the Romantic movement in the arts, so it was necessary, I suppose, for him to write in the flowery way he did; but it is ironic that he was so heavy and unattractive in his personal appearance, and, although till his last breath he declared Carlotta Grisi to be the real love of his life, he married and settled down to having a family with her sister. Not very romantic, I would say! Nevertheless, he did leave us a truly Romantic ballet for which all ballerinas must bless his memory. He collaborated on the scenario of *Giselle,* written especially for his love Carlotta. The ballet combined an Elssler-type girl in Act I and a Taglioni-type spirit in Act II, which conveniently gave Grisi the opportunity to supplant them both at once in their absence—the one in America, the other in Russia.

The use of seemingly magical illusions like flying in the air or disappearing through

the floor was common practice in all eighteenth- and nineteenth-century theatre, and essential to Romantic ballet. Usually it was superbly well done, but never without some risk for the performers. In one of Taglioni's Paris performances, two sylphs were suspended in the air on wires that jammed and would neither raise them up nor lower them down until a stagehand managed to descend dangerously on a rope to set them free. On another occasion, during *Giselle* in Brussels, three of the corps de ballet suffered a horrible accident as they waited to make their entrance from below. Before the section of stage above their heads had slid to one side, opening the trap through which they were to appear, the stagehand controlling a counterweight unfortunately let go of the rope, and the platform on which they stood shot up with such velocity that they suffered severe damage to their heads and arms. Ladies in the audience inevitably screamed when disasters occurred or were anticipated, but there was reputedly a young English nobleman of such ghoulish tastes that he sat through every performance of *La Péri* just for the thrill of Carlotta Grisi's spectacular leap from a high platform into her partner's arms. He was sure she would kill herself one night and he didn't want to miss it.

The Romantic ballet era, which lasted hardly more than twenty years, came and went in the middle of the brief interlude between candle-light and electricity. The stopgap was gas lighting, a soft glowing illumination that enhanced the magic of the delicate sylphs while endangering their lives with its hard jet of flame that set fire so much more readily than the weaker flame of a candle—and that was dangerous enough in theatres built mainly of wood. The Paris Opera had burnt down once in 1771 and again ten years later. There is a gruesome description of the second fire:

MLLE. GUIMARD

A candle on a side piece had set light to a border cloth. Water was at once called for, but none was available. There were shouts to cut the ropes which sustained, the border, but this was done on one side only, the wrong side, and the cloth, assuming a perpendicular position, gave added strength and fuel to the flames, which, running up the backcloth, spread to the centre and then to all the borders with the utmost rapidity . . . the stagehands and actors . . . driven back by the smoke, sought safety in flight. The flames had already cut off the retreat of all those who were not on the stage.

The dancer Dangui, three tailors, and six stagehands were burnt to ashes. Beaupré . . . leaped from the third storey and was killed; one of his colleagues, taking the same course, broke his thigh. Huard, a tall, muscular dancer, having only two storeys to clear, leaped towards the roof of a shop, slipped into the Cour des Fontaines and alighted on his feet without hurt. His servant, a boy of fifteen, remained at the window and feared to make the jump. Huard holds out his arms, calling to him, encourages him, saying that he is ready to catch him and break his fall. But nothing would induce the unfortunate boy to take the leap, not even the flames, which soon reached him, and burnt him alive before his master's eyes. Mademoiselle Guimard, fully undressed, without a chemise on her body, stifled and grilled in her dressing room and did not dare to move. A stagehand ran to her assistance, wrapped her up in some curtains and carried her through the whirlwinds of smoke and flame.

The rescued lady was Madeleine Guimard, a famous ballerina nicknamed the "Skeleton of the Graces" because she was so small and thin that when she danced a pas de trois with two tall men, a wit said they looked like two dogs fighting over a bone. Her technique was limited, but she put so much feeling, grace, and charm into everything she did that the public preferred her to all other dancers—and for longer. It was said that at forty-five she looked no more than fifteen on the stage, owing to the fact that, when she was young she had a portrait made, and for the rest of her life never went out in the morning without spending an hour or two in her boudoir reproducing the exact tones and shades of the portrait on her own face.

She must have had all the fascination of Mathilde Kschessinskaya and a very similar life. Both of them had rich, influential lovers, both had palaces built for them, both lived through violent revolutions, losing all possessions and ending up in Paris happily married—Guimard to the ballet master Despréaux, for whom she renounced her career because the church would neither marry or bury anyone involved with the stage.

ONE OF MANY FIRES AT THE PARIS OPERA

EMMA LIVRY IN *HERCULANUM*

When Guimard died in 1816, gas lighting had shone on the streets of London for nine years. When Kschessinskaya was born in 1872, electricity was soon to reach the streets of New York. In the intervening years, tragic accidents took the lives of two young ballerinas, each a great loss to her own country. Clara Webster, trained by her father and partnered by her brother, was one of the few very talented English ballerinas. She was only twenty-three when her costume caught fire before the eyes of the public during a performance at Drury Lane in 1844. A stagehand rushed out from the wings and threw himself on her without a thought for his own safety, and a doctor in the audience tended her in the Green Room with "the usual applications of spirits of wine, water, flour, etc. . . ." But in spite of everything they could do, she died within three days.

Even more harrowing was the fate of Emma Livry in Paris on November 15th, 1862. There are many ironies to her accident, the greatest being that electricity was already in use in some theatres although to a very limited extent. Another irony was that the government had issued a decree, almost three years earlier, calling for the fireproofing of all scenery and costumes. Unfortunately, the process, which treated materials chemically, was

LIVRY'S FATAL PERFORMANCE IN *LA MUETTE DE PORTICI*, NOVEMBER 15, 1862

particularly unfavourable to the dancers' white skirts, taking away their airy quality and leaving them dingy. There is almost nothing worse on stage than to feel unattractively dressed, so some dancers ignored the regulation. You may wonder why they would risk so horrible a death, but you may as well ask yourself why anyone travels on the roads. Life is full of risks. Emma wrote to the director of the Opera on September 23rd, 1860:

> *I insist, sir, on dancing at all first performances of the ballet in my ordinary ballet skirt, and I take upon myself all responsibility for anything that may occur. In the last scene I am willing to dance in a treated skirt, but I cannot wear skirts which will be ugly, or which will not become me. However, as I feel that the management is quite right to bring into force the proposed alterations, I will myself ask after a few performances, for a substitution to be made, provided that it will not spoil the effect of the costume, which is what I fear. With best wishes, Emma Livry.*

Emma had been an exceptional student and made her first appearance not in the corps de ballet, as would be usual, but, helped by her mother's influential lover who ar-

231

EMMA LIVRY

ranged the matter with the Opera director, in the title role of *La Sylphide*, which was incredibly daring for a début. Marie Taglioni came out of retirement and returned to Paris to see this sixteen-year-old who was causing such a sensation in her own great role, and recognized something of herself in the girl, who was certainly not beautiful but had a pure nature and extreme lightness in her dancing; Marie took her under her wing and choreographed a ballet, *Le Papillon*, especially for her. For the première she sent Emma a photograph inscribed with the message: "Make me forgotten, but do not forget me." In fact, Emma was amazingly reminiscent of Marie and revived old memories. A critic wrote:

> *For this role, so ethereal and so diaphanous, an intangible artiste is imperative, an artiste with whom ballon is a natural gift, and Mademoiselle Emma Livry has a ballon which has never been equalled . . . she skims over the ground, the water, and the flowers, apparently without touching them. She rises like a feather, and falls like a snowflake.*

Emma was eighteen when she created *Le Papillon*, in which as a butterfly she is consumed by a flame but magically restored. She was twenty in 1862 when her costume caught fire at the final rehearsal of an opera, *La Muette de Portici*. She had gone down to the stage early and sat in the wings, listening to the tenor. As she rose to prepare for her entrance she shook out her skirts, as ballerinas always do without thinking, but it was just one little second of carelessness—she was too near a gas jet. The movement of air caused the flame to reach out and catch her skirt. Almost instantly she was in the centre of a column of flame, "walking amid fire," as she ran onto the stage in panic. A fireman ran to her with a blanket, turning her upside down to save her face and head. As soon as the flames were stifled, she was seen struggling to her knees. She was trying to pray. One of the newspaper reports said:

On seeing the dangerous plight of their friend, all the young members of the ballet went into hysterics.

This emotion is explained by the interest taken in the graceful talent and virtuous and amiable character of Mademoiselle Livry.

First aid was rendered by Doctor Laborie and Doctor Renegaud, who were present at the rehearsal. The burns, although superficial, are dangerous on account of their extent.

How sad these words are when we know the outcome! For eight long months she endured agony, showing extraordinary fortitude in her suffering, only to die on July 26th, 1863. She was twenty. A huge crowd came to her funeral and Théophile Gautier recounts that "Two white butterflies did not cease from circling over the white coffin during its journey from the church to the cemetery."

There is a story that a popular author had once asked Emma's help with some backstage material for a new novel. When he called upon her to give his thanks, she said, "At least tell me the story of your book." After he had finished she was very thoughtful for a moment or two, then turned to her mother and said, "To be burned to death, that must be very painful," and added, "All the same, it is a fine death for a dancer."

Had Emma lived, I think she would have been the missing link between Taglioni and Pavlova. They were the Three Graces of Dance, each one slender with long, narrow feet and the air of another world clinging about her frail form. If one remembers that the first homes of ballet were Italy, France, and Russia, and that Taglioni was Italian by her father, and Pavlova purely Russian, surely Emma Livry would have been the true representative of France, the country where ballet was born, and where Romantic ballet was born. How could France have gone through the whole nineteenth century without producing one native ballerina of international class equal to Taglioni?

Emma's name is on a tomb in the Cimetière de Montmartre not far from that of Théophile Gautier. By the time he died, barely ten years later, all his beloved sylphs had flown out the window; they were, in any case, far too insubstantial for opulent late-nineteenth-century tastes. "Art for art's sake," Gautier's favourite phrase, had given way to art for pleasure's sake, and the romanticism he loved so much was replaced by mere frivolity. Who was interested in wraiths? Nearly fifty years were to pass before the forgotten sylphs, who had flown off to distant Russia, would return, suddenly and unexpectedly, to ensnare the willing Parisians once again and divert them with beauty and poetry.

The 1860's in Paris saw stars of the dance who were quite different in style from the ladies of the ballet. These were the high kickers, and they inhabited the slopes of Montmartre, where the cancan and the chahut expressed the youthful tastes and high spirits of the day. The Opera had its own public; it was practically a club whose patrons went to see each other and to be seen, to gossip, flirt, make assignations, and, incidentally, enjoy moments

AN EA

of the performances. The people who went to Montmartre went simply to have a good time and enjoy the exhilarating abandon of their favourite stars, such as Céleste Mogador and Rose Ponpon. Here, it was the young artists, students, and shopgirls who were in their element, far from the frowsty institutions of the "establishment."

Twenty years later, in the 1880's, the cancan was even wilder and its stars more famous, with their piquant stage names that evoke Paris at its naughtiest. La Goulue,

Grille d'Egout, and Nini Pattes-en-l'Air were among those who were known far and wide and whom gentlemen of the highest rank were amused to take to supper. Undoubtedly they were passionate, uninhibited, undisciplined, natural dancers. The music had only to start up and they were possessed by demons, their heads thrown about, their bodies gyrating, and their legs kicking high in the sky.

NCAN

La Goulue was small and delicately made with ivory shoulders and golden hair. She was well aware of her charms and audacious in the frenzy of her dancing. Grille d'Egout was dark, excessively thin, and quite unattractive in repose, but a mad gaiety took hold of her waif-like figure the minute she began to move. As for Nini Pattes-en-l'Air, she was the strangest of them all, with black hair and deathly white face. Her dancing was wild and fast, her legs disjointed, her movements unpredictable and without logic as though electric currents ran through her body. These dancers were very much a part of fin-de-siècle Paris with the luxury of its boulevards and the ferment of its artistic life, which unfortunately did not extend to ballet at the Opera.

The one bright spark from this period is *Coppélia,* created in 1870 during the Franco-Prussian War. It has music by Delibes that is perfectly right, and a plot light as a child's balloon but firmly tethered to the superb central character of Dr. Coppélius, the toy-maker, who can be sinister, tragic, or hilariously funny. Franz, the young male lead, was danced by Mlle. Fiocre, a great beauty with long legs and a ready wit—at the Opera this role continued to be interpreted by females until the 1950's—and as there was no French dancer with the right technique and personality to play the mischievous heroine, Swanilda, it was given to a sixteen-year-old Italian, Giuseppina Bozzacchi, her first starring role. The ballet was choreographed by Arthur Saint-Léon, the violinist-dancer. Within a few months he and Bozzacchi were dead, he from a heart attack at forty-nine, and she from a virulent fever caught during the siege of Paris, when the inhabitants had no fuel, and a dog or cat for dinner was a treat—even a rat was hard to come by. Giuseppina was too young to withstand the privations on top of the hard work she had put into *Coppélia;* the fever took her life on the day she turned seventeen.

CANCAN DANCERS AT THE MOULIN ROUGE

SAHARET: CANCAN HIGH-KICKER

GIUSEPPINA BOZZACCHI IN *COPPELIA*

CARLOTTA ZAMBELLI IN *GISELLE*

PIERINA LEGNANI IN *SWAN LAKE*

CARLOTTA BRIANZA IN *THE SLEEPING BEAUTY*

Bozzacchi had an unusually strong technique because she was from Milan and had begun her training there. For the next twenty-five years almost every top ballerina in every opera house in Europe came from the school of La Scala Theatre in Milan, where the system laid down in the 1830's by Carlo Blasis was very advanced, especially in the development of dancing on the toes. The products of his method were able to do many new and difficult steps not seen elsewhere, and they were greatly in demand everywhere. Even in Russia, sturdy Carlotta Brianza was the first Princess Aurora in *The Sleeping Beauty,* and dumpy Pierina Legnani danced Odette-Odile in the *Swan Lake* of 1895. Both were impressive, but hardly ethereal. In order to show off their virtuosity, ballerinas of the period shortened their skirts—otherwise their legs would hardly have been seen at all—so the soft, full ballet skirt Marie Taglioni had introduced climbed to just below the knee, then to mid-thigh. As it was shortened, it was made fuller and stood out more and more stiffly until it became the modern ballet tutu.

One thing all the Italian ballerinas had was strength. Tamara Karsavina recalled going to Milan as a young dancer in 1904 to study with Caterina Beretta, who was over sixty when Karsavina called on her in her apartment to arrange about the lessons: "A ludicrous little figure waddled in. Fat and short, her pyramidal shape was emphasized by a

LES SYLPHIDES: TAMARA KARSAVINA *(Left),* ANNA PAVLOVA

very small head with a meagre blob of hair on top. From the look of her it was impossible that she should have been a great star of the Scala." Karsavina found the classes killing, but they greatly improved her stamina, and, like Taglioni after her father's lessons, or Pavlova after two years with Cecchetti, Karsavina became a peerless ballerina.

So one can see how it happened that the Russians learned all there was to know about ballet first from the French and then from the Italians, and added some magic of

TH KARSAVINA, 1909

their own, until they reached the greatest height of grandeur and virtuosity. Then there came a day when they looked back to the pure simplicity of Taglioni and, in 1909, sent to Paris a ballet called *Les Sylphides*. Once again the dancers floated through moonbeams in soft tarlatan skirts with wings at their backs and wreaths of flowers on their heads; and I can't help thinking that, in his grave by Lake Como, Filippo may have been gently muttering, "Didn't I say so long ago?"

DANCE MYTHOLOGICAL

Magnificence, extravagance, artificiality, a tiny society in which everyone knew every detail of everyone else's life—that was the court of Louis XIV, the Sun King, and it was into that world that professional ballet was born. For Louis was an accomplished dancer and appeared in many court "ballets" from the age of twelve until he was thirty-two, when affairs of state and his sense of royal dignity made him give them up—he had grown rather fat—although he continued to perform his favourite ballroom dances.

The performance that identified him with his popular image was *Le Ballet de la Nuit*, when he was fourteen, in which his last entrance—near the end of the thirteen-hour performance—showed him as the Rising Sun accompanied by Honour, Grace, Love, Riches, Victory, Fame, and Peace. The allegory was apt, for he was indeed as brilliant and powerful as the sun, and he was to bring honour, grace, victory, and fame to France. Among his famous achievements, and still France's finest showpiece, is the Palace of Versailles, where he would give fêtes lasting two or three days at a time, with plays, ballets, banquets, fireworks, and all kinds of imaginative diversions for which special theatres and halls were improvised among the magnificent gardens. He was well aware of the restrictions of court life and took pains to amuse his courtiers and, perhaps, to keep them out of mischief and intrigue. And, of course, he loved the entertainments himself.

What an incredible man he was! Tall and vigorous, he lived to be seventy-seven with hardly a day's illness in his life (which was lucky in an age when there were no anaesthetics, and doctors had not even thought of washing their hands before operating). He was a great statesman, a man of vision, a fine soldier, art connoisseur, and sportsman; and, as he was king from the age of five, he reigned for seventy-two years—from 1643 to 1715. It does seem strange to me that the history books rarely speak of what he did for ballet; they hardly mention his enthusiasm for dancing, although his was a time when grace was a manly virtue and it was only to be expected that, being a perfectionist in everything he

Opposite: LOUIS XIV AS THE SUN KING IN *LE BALLET DE LA NUIT,* 1653

touched, he would express grace in all his movements.

In 1661 Louis grew impatient with the endless bickering among leading dancing masters, and set up an academy in which he hoped they would work together to amalgamate and codify their knowledge. In the letters patent establishing the academy he stated his views thus:

> *The art of dance has ever been acknowledged to be one of the most suitable and necessary arts for physical development and for affording the primary and most natural preparation for all bodily exercises, and among others, those concerning the use of weapons, and consequently it is one of the most valuable and most useful arts for nobles and others who have the honour to enter our presence not only in time of war in our armies, but even in time of peace in our ballets.*

Clearly he was very serious. Every movement he made was carefully studied. For example, he doffed his hat to all ladies, and for the highest male dignitaries he dislodged it as far as one ear, but for lesser beings merely touched it with his hand. The ladies, too, were expected to be equally fastidious about the accurate depth of their curtseys. Seemingly minor points were taken so seriously that their infringement could bring dramatic conse-

FIREWORKS AT THE PALACE OF VERSAILLES

quences. The famous chef Le Grand Vatel committed suicide because a dinner he had prepared for the king's visit to his master's house failed Vatel's own high expectations.

This curious mixture of artistic refinement and artificiality made everyday life a kind of theatre on its own, but a theatre with amateur limitations. Louis, with his usual perspicacity, saw that the possibilities of dance exceeded these bounds and, realizing that it could progress no further as an amateur pastime, established the Académie Royale de Musique—which passed through some changes of title too complicated to go into, but is generally known as the Paris Opera—where his favourite dancing master, Pierre Beauchamp, directed the first professional school and ballet company. Its original home was in a large covered building in the rue Vaugirard, suitably shaped for a theatre and described as an abandoned tennis court.

For all his wisdom and foresight, I cannot help imagining how surprised Louis would have been if he could have looked ahead three hundred years and seen how that little seed, planted by him in 1669, would flower and spread all across the world—even to far Cathay. The Chinese emperor would have been even more astonished to know that Peking would one day have its own ballet company, performing steps with French names that were in common usage long before Louis' reign.

BALLET DIVERTISSEMENT IN THE MARBLE COURTYARD AT VERSAILLES

YEW TREE BALL IN THE HAL

MIRRORS AT VERSAILLES

Two definitions of dance, one written fifty years before Louis was born and the other shortly after his death, show how his influence helped to make order out of confusion. In 1588 Thoinot Arbeau, who was a precise-minded dancing master, published a book of carefully detailed social dances with full instructions. But when he came to define dancing, this was the best he could do:

> *Dancing, so to speak, is to jump, to hop, to prance, to sway, to tread, to tiptoe, and to move the feet, hands, and body in certain rhythms, measures, and movements consisting of jumps, bendings of the body, straddlings, limpings, bendings of the knees, risings on tiptoe, throwings-forward of the feet, changes and other movements.*

By 1721 John Weaver in London was able to give this definition:

> *Dancing is an elegant and regular movement, harmonically composed of beautiful attitudes and contrasted graceful postures of the body, and parts thereof.*

NAVAL SCENE FROM A SPECTACLE, PRESENTED INSIDE TURIN CASTLE, 1628

For the first hundred years of professional ballet, its centre of development remained firmly in Paris, where Louis had placed it. In those early days ballet was a new theatre art only remotely aware of its potential to exploit the physical capabilities of its exponents. The figurative and literal heights to which a Nijinsky or a Nureyev would soar could not be foreseen as long as dancers wore heeled shoes with buckles and noblemen could still join with professionals in a performance at the new Opera.

One must go back a little in time to see what forms "ballet" had passed through in its evolution to the point where Louis set it free on its course as a full-fledged art. At first it was only social dancing and very formal, although some dances like "La Volta" were decidedly spirited. Here the man lifted his partner into the air with one hand under her seat and whirled her around; it was so risqué that the young folk usually waited until their elders had gone to bed before dancing it far into the night. Before panties, knickers, bloomers, drawers, or pantaloons came into fashion, the least flick of a skirt above the ankle sent everyone into a tizzy of apprehension. For special festivities in courts or castles, the social dances were arranged into little interludes interspersing the recital of poetry in a sort of "cabaret" performance—simply a series of unconnected items.

The next stage of development was an entertainment on a single theme; the separate items were linked together to tell a single story, and the "cabaret" form of entertainment evolved into the "musical." The man responsible for this new conception was an Italian musician invited to France by Catherine de' Médici when she became queen. His cumbersome name was Baldassarino di Belgiojoso; when he settled in France he changed it to Balthasar de Beaujoyeulx to make it easier! Just as Marius Petipa later went from France to

A BALL GIVEN BY THE DUKE OF JOYEUSE, 1581

develop ballet in Russia, and Balanchine from Russia to America, so Beaujoyeulx took the original court ballets from Italy to France and started the pattern of transporting ballet from one country to another. Beaujoyeulx published a libretto to explain his *Ballet Comique de la Reine,* given at the Louvre in 1581, in which he described it as a modern invention because he mingled music, poetry, and dance to make the dance speak and the music sing, satisfying, as he put it, "the eye, the ear, and the intellect."

Men like Beaujoyeulx were musician, choreographer, producer, and director combined. Their imagination for the spectacular was unlimited, but was always put to the service of allegorical and mythological subjects. Sixty years after the *Ballet Comique de la Reine,* a M. de St. Hubert was advocating the search for fresh ideas; but when someone suggested Homer's *Iliad,* he was scathing:

> *I told him frankly that it would be a play rather than a ballet, that the ceilings of the halls were too low for the masts of Greek vessels, that the horses of Hector's chariot, if frightened, might injure people, and that the burning of Troy would scare the ladies.*

Even when ballet moved into professional theatre, mythological subjects still prevailed for a long time, but the technique of movement took wings. Two male dancers at the Paris Opera, Jean Balon and Nicolas Blondy, performed the usual social dance steps with an agility and abandon that would have looked vulgar in a ballroom but were thrilling on the stage. Balon is pictured with elegant figure and well-turned-out legs. He has such an air of distinction that one is not at all surprised to know he was permitted to shake hands with Louis XIV and keep his hat on in the royal presence as a mark of the king's admiration. Only one other person in ordinary life shared this honour, and that was the gardener, Le Nôtre, who landscaped Versailles.

Dancers were strictly categorized according to their physique: the Louis XIV type—tall, well built, with good legs—was a danseur noble. Such was Balon. These men danced the slow controlled steps requiring lightness and precision, modelling themselves on the Sun King himself, who, it is said, relished his own excellence so much in the Slow Courante that he repeated it over and over, more and more slowly, until his court, in the

LA VOLTA DANCED AT A BALL AT THE COURT OF THE VALOIS

MONSIEUR BALON

extremes of boredom, could hardly keep awake. The dancers of the second category, called demi-caractères, were of more compact physique. They concentrated their efforts on jumps and quick movements in which they showed themselves to great advantage. They were the virtuosi. In the last category were the danseurs comiques, and they were stockily built. Their roles were energetic and humorous, sometimes styled as "grotesques."

Louis Dupré was the first danseur noble in Paris to be dubbed the "God of Dance" because of his perfect physique and refined style. There is a story that Dupré started out as a violinist. One day during a rehearsal, a young dancer insulted Dupré's playing. Dupré responded that the dancer should take up the violin, because his dancing was abominable. The dancer suggested that *both* of them might do better if they exchanged professions, which they did on the spot—and the dancer Leclair became as famous a violinist as Dupré a dancer. Casanova, the much-travelled notorious lover and writer, was taken to the Paris Opera in 1750, a year before Dupré retired, and described the evening in his memoirs. Being Italian, he lost no opportunity to point out the errors of the French and, as soon as the curtain rose on the opera *Les Fêtes Vénitiennes,* he noticed a "comical an disgraceful mistake." The doge's palace in Venice was on the wrong side of the Cam-

COSTUME DESIGN FOR A DEMON,
LATE 17th CENTURY

panile! After some criticisms of the music he continued:

> *It was a truly curious sight for a Venetian, when I saw the Doge, attended by twelve Councillors, appear on the stage, all dressed in the most odd cloaks and dancing a "grand passacaille." Suddenly the pit gave vent to a loud clapping of hands at the appearance of a tall, well-proportioned dancer, wearing a mask and an enormous black wig, the ends of which were half-way down his back, dressed in a robe, open in front and reaching to his heels. My friend said, "It is the inimitable Dupré. . . ."*
>
> *I saw that fine figure coming forward with measured step, and when the dancer had arrived in front of the stage, he slowly raised his rounded and graceful arms, opened, extended and closed them, moved his feet with precision and lightness, took a few small steps, made some "battements" and "pirouettes" and disappeared like a summer breeze. The whole had not lasted more than half a minute. Applause and shouts burst from every part of the house. I was astonished and asked my friend the reason for it. He replied, "We applaud the grace of Dupré and the divine harmony of his movements. He is now sixty years old and those who saw him forty years ago say that he is always the same."*

MLLE. DE LA FONTAINE

At the end of the second act Dupré made another appearance, dressed the same way, and danced to a different tune, "but, in my opinion," wrote Casanova, "doing exactly the same thing."

In view of the wig and mask, it must have been quite difficult to move at all. Apparently the masks were desirable because lighting was so poor and make-up inadequate. Also, men danced the male and female roles for the first nine years at the Opera, since court ladies, who had often danced in royal entertainments, could not possibly be seen on a public stage, and there were as yet no trained professionals.

The first ballerina to appear was Mlle. de la Fontaine, who was twenty-six when she danced at the converted tennis court in the rue Vaugirard. Unfortunately, very little is known about her except that she was born in 1655, danced at the Opera for nine years, was called the Queen of Dance, and retired to a nunnery, where she lived for another fifty years—praying, one would hope, for the morals of her successors. She herself was a modest, virtuous lady—at least one presumes she was since the scandalmongers could find no excuse to attack her—she must have been out of place in the rowdy rough-and-tumble of the theatre at the time; no wonder she retired young.

Theatre patrons, sitting in an ill-lit house on hard seats, felt entitled to enjoy themselves in whatever way the mood took them, which, since half of them were drunk, was

MLLE. SUBLIGNY

usually by adding bawdy words to the songs onstage and loudly praising or criticizing the performers not only for their art—or lack of it—but for their appearance and morals as well. No doubt the occasional dog brought into the audience added a few barks to the uproar and the candles some of the patrons held for warmth and illumination scorched their clothing if they didn't actually start minor fires. The smell and the scratching must have been appalling.

In the Foyer de la Danse of the present Paris Opera, opened in 1875, there are twenty portraits of ballerinas; they decorate the plasterwork near the ceiling, forming a kind of coronet around the ornate room, which is just behind the stage. One wall is completely mirror-lined and the floor slopes to the same angle as the stage for the convenience of dancers practising and warming up. Mlle. de la Fontaine's picture is centred over the entrance opposite the mirror-wall. The last in the series is Carolina Rosati, Italian by birth, who in 1856 danced in the very first production of *Le Corsaire*, the ballet now best known for its sensational pas de deux re-choreographed in St. Petersburg in 1899 and made famous in the West by Rudolf Nureyev.

Mlle. de la Fontaine's first name is unknown, but her successor in the next portrait compensates for that shortcoming with the name of Marie-Thérèse Perdou de Subligny. With her pretty figure and expressive eyes, she reigned at the Opera for seventeen years,

MLLE. MOREAU

MLLE. MAUPAIN

MLLE. SUBLIGNY

MLLE. HURETTI

and was the first French ballerina to dance in England. The next in succession is Françoise Prévost, elegant, graceful, light, and quite an innovator in that she extended her art to silent acting. She expressed "the manners and passions of mankind" in dance and mime so effectively that she had her audience in tears.

"La Camargo" and Marie Sallé come next. They were contrasting rivals, as Taglioni and Elssler would be later. Camargo, like Taglioni the daughter of an Italian dancing master who gave her a prodigious technique, made her Opera début at sixteen and became a star at once. She was short and not pretty, but charm and vivacity made up for those defects, and she is famous for having shortened her large pannier skirts to a little above the ankle to give a clear view of her twinkling entrechats—a step previously done only by men. Casanova wrote about her: "I saw a danseuse who bounded like a fury, cutting entrechats to the right and left and in all directions, but scarcely rising from the ground; yet she was received with fervent applause." Camargo's gaiety, which made her so loved on stage, vanished as soon as she reached the wings, when her natural melancholy took over.

Marie Sallé was different in every way. Her childhood was spent with her touring theatrical family of players, clowns, and tumblers, who performed each summer at the big Paris street fairs. Marie showed so much talent for dancing that her parents sent her to study with Françoise Prévost and she made her début at the Opera one year after Camargo. Paris was quick to stir up a rivalry between the two, the one a brilliant technician, the other an outstanding dancer-actress. Camargo had many rich lovers, which was exactly what was expected of a ballerina, but Sallé was interested only in the world of artists and intellectuals. Handel composed a short ballet for her, Voltaire was among her friends. She was always a nonconformist, creating ballets that were ahead of her time. She would have revelled in Ulanova's role of Juliet. For her ballet on Pygmalion, she caused a stir by wearing a light muslin dress instead of the usual heavy costume with boned bodice. London was more receptive to her free spirit than was Paris, and she returned often to the city where she had first achieved a great success at the age of twelve, dancing with her brother at Lincoln's Inn Fields.

Another among the portraits in the Foyer de la Danse is Thérèse Vestris, who was a terrible dancer and, as she could hardly have been selected for having more lovers than all the others counted together, the only possible explanation is because her brother and nephew were the two most illustrious male dancers of the eighteenth and nineteenth centuries. They were Gaetano Vestris and his son Auguste.

They were one of the big dancing families, Italians from Florence. I can imagine that when Gaetano arrived at the Opera as a tall, very handsome foreigner, and talented too, he encountered jealousy and spite. He probably decided attack was the best form of defense and developed a flamboyant ego, which, with his personal magnetism, was the very stuff to delight Paris. He could get away with anything and was soon renowned equally for his dancing and his quips, which I suspect were made tongue in cheek to foster his reputation for outrageous vanity. His best remark was in reference to his son's extraordinary talent. He said, "The reason he is a greater dancer than I is simple. He has Gaetano Vestris for his father. That is a gift nature denied to me."

Auguste inherited his father's reputation for vanity, and in his case it was almost certainly justified. For one thing, he had seen how the image helped his father, and for another, he had a more difficult start in life, being the illegitimate son of the dancer Marie Allard. She was so promiscuous that when young Vestris made his first success on the stage, Jean Dauberval, standing in the wings, was able to joke, "I missed being the father of that great talent by only fifteen minutes." Auguste's parentage was known to everyone—

LA CAMARGO

MARIE SALLÉ

GAETANO VESTRIS AS THE PRINCE IN *NINETTE À LA COUR*

for a while he was called Vestr'Allard—so the poor boy had to live up to his father's fame and live down his mother's reputation. He succeeded admirably in both.

During Gaetano's career, heavy wigs and masks finally went out of favour. It all began one night when Gaetano was ill and could not appear, and the dancer called to replace him agreed only on condition that he could go on without the obligatory mask so the audience would recognize who he was. Auguste and his generation were the beneficiaries of this breaking of a convention that had persisted for almost a hundred years. Auguste danced in light clothing with a small wig. He could spin until no one could count how

AUGUSTE VESTRIS AS COLAS IN *NINETTE À LA COUR*

many turns he made, and he could jump in the air as though jet-propelled. It did not matter that he was short and knock-kneed, or even that he lacked the gracious style of his father. People watching him were amazed that neither dizziness nor gravity had their normal power over him as he forced virtuosity to levels unimagined. Paris declared him the ultimate God of Dance. He initiated an era comparable to the present day, when Nureyev and Baryshnikov have set standards that could not have been foreseen twenty years ago, but with the difference that we now see refinement and virtuosity combined—a projection of both Vestrises in one.

GAETANO VESTRIS IN *JASON ET MEDÉE*

Auguste lived from 1760 to 1842. He saw the progression from Dupré, in his huge wig, to Taglioni, on one toe. Everything from Auguste Vestris on belongs to ballet as we know it, everything before him belongs to the world of magnificence, extravagance, and artificiality—to Europe before the French Revolution. To have a sense of what it must have been like living in that world, or at least the more pleasurable side of that life, there is nowhere more evocative than the little royal theatre at Drottningholm in Sweden. The story of this enchanting place, which sits beside a palace in a tranquil stretch of parkland, is improbable and wonderful.

In 1792, after King Gustaf III's assassination at a masked ball in Stockholm, the theatre was closed, and somehow forgotten, for over one hundred years—but how can a building be forgotten? When it was rediscovered in 1921, thick with dust and cobwebs, nothing had been touched since the end of the eighteenth century, and one can still see the original candleholders for stage illumination, the original machinery for scene changes, the original floorboards, and the platforms that lowered people from the skies amid painted clouds. Perhaps the greatest treasures are the thirty sets of original scenery.

CUPID OUT OF HIS HUMOUR, A MYTHOLOGICAL BALLET, DROTTNINGHOLM COURT THEATRE

The theatre is small, yet its proportions make it astonishingly spacious and it exudes an agreeable atmosphere of comfort and warmth. One can easily imagine a group of actors, perhaps from France, who have set out with the first hint of spring to travel north, stopping from time to time to perform for private patrons or in public theatres, reaching Sweden as the king and his court moved out to their summer residence. The players, with children, costumes, props, and baggage, are engaged for the season; and where should they lodge but right in the theatre? Above the cozy dressing rooms are pleasant apartments looking out over the sun-lit sweep of park with its trees and lakes. Money had run short as the theatre was being built, so silk or cloth was too costly for the walls. Instead, each room has its hand-painted eighteenth-century wallpaper.

For the children brought up in those surroundings, in that busy self-sufficient little world of acting, dancing, tumbling, music, and the art and craft of theatre, it must have been a gloriously happy life. If they were lucky, they might have got an occasional pat on the head from the king as he breakfasted with the troupe in a marble foyer added especially for that purpose.

Gustaf III was a great patron who loved theatre and encouraged many Swedish artists. He it was who had sent young Didelot to train in Paris after picking him out for his brilliant play-acting of a monkey at a costume ball. Among Didelot's teachers was Jean Dauberval, who at eighteen had narrowly missed becoming the father of Auguste Vestris. He is best known now for his ballet *La Fille Mal Gardée,* although we no longer see his version, which has been lost in the mists of time. Its première was at Bordeaux in 1789, on the eve of the French Revolution. As the son of an actor, Dauberval had a wider view of ballet as a theatre art than the more purely dance-oriented choreographers, and he loved stories of historic events or very human people.

In *La Fille Mal Gardée,* the widow of a well-to-do farmer has promised her daughter to the son of a prosperous landowner. The boy turns out to be a half-wit, and the daughter is determined to marry the young neighbour she loves, but the mother is equally determined to keep them apart. With these characters, Dauberval made a refreshingly humorous and touching ballet that has remained a gift to all dancers; there is something in it for everyone.

MARIE ALLARD AND JEAN DAUBERVAL IN *SILVIE*, C. 1767

THE INSPIRATION FOR DAUBERVAL'S *LA FILLE MAL GARDÉE*

THE DANCING MASTER, 1745

Didelot danced it and produced it in Russia, Viganò staged it in Venice, Auguste Vestris danced it in London when he was fifty-five, Filippo Taglioni danced it and added a pas de trois for Marie. Fanny Elssler was superb as the young girl, Virginia Zucchi was even better, Karsavina was enchanting, and Pavlova adorable.

Dauberval was one of the great choreographers and a fine dancer too; he was tall, good-looking, brimming over with vitality, an extrovert with a warm personality and no patience with those who opposed him. He was frequently at cross-purposes with his theatre directors, and he knew when he was right. If he could have chosen one choreographer of our own century to re-create his greatest ballet, it would have been Frederick Ashton, I am sure, and he would be delighted if he could see Ashton's version, which was first performed in 1960. It is a triumphant masterpiece, the perfect ballet.

Of all the collection of vital, energetic, rambunctious personalities who lived, loved, and squabbled their way through the French Revolution, Dauberval seems to have been the most intellectually attuned to the greater significance of events outside the Opera ambiance. There must have been quite a few who couldn't, and would not have wanted to, adapt themselves to a changed world. They lived in the cherished past, like the society dancing master M. Abraham:

> *Imbued with the importance of his art and his sacred memories of the French Court before the revolution, proud of having taught French graces to that beautiful Marie Antoinette of whom he obligingly quoted several Austrian awkwardnesses during his first lessons; prouder still of being the only one to preserve the great . . . Menuet with the correct interpretation and graduated pliés of the révérence, M. Abraham held himself in high honour. He never visited the houses of his noble pupils except in a carriage and attired in full dress. He entered and departed, sat down and rose, spoke, scolded, coughed and blew his nose, always in the most ceremonious manner. The fingers that he rested on the bow of his little violin were covered with enormous diamonds, each of which, so he said, had been given to him by some Queen or Princess Royal. From his hoary wig to the gilt buckles on his dancing shoes, from his fine lace jabot to the black silk stockings drawn tightly over his false calves, everything in him aimed at majesty of demeanour. His steps, when he executed them before parents—he never took this trouble for a mere pupil—displayed a consummate precision and ease.*

M. Abraham, still clinging to his absurdly out-of-date knee breeches, padded calves, and gilt shoe buckles, represented the last vestiges of mythological entertainments and the origins of ballet, which, without the imagination of a king who was wealthy and wise, might never have been born at all.

In our day and age, with its shortage of kings and support for the arts so costly, some help from the state is necessary, but it is noticeable that many of the events in this century that have brought dance to pre-eminence happened without a whiff of interest, let alone money, from the state—at least not until they were already well established. One can list Pavlova, Duncan, and dozens of other recitalists; Diaghilev and a Swedish off-shoot called Les Ballets Suédois; the Germans led by Kurt Jooss; the British, the post-war French, American, Australian, Japanese, and many more besides—all of whom have had to make their own way to success. There is still no such thing as an American national opera and ballet, yet New York is the current mecca for all dancers. Surely there is a moral in this.

With a combination of private and state funds, American dance has managed to prosper artistically and develop better than the purely state-run companies. For some obscure reason it is difficult to channel the most original innovative talents through firmly established organizations. Diaghilev could never have achieved his miracle at the Imperial Theatre or the Paris Opera, because such organizations tend to settle too comfortably into inflexible routines.

The single enlightened art patron is ideal but no longer feasible; yet two people did succeed, by sheer purposeful effort, in raising American ballet to its present high level.

The first is Lucia Chase, originally a dancer, who has dedicated herself and much of her fortune to building and shaping American Ballet Theatre into the most "national" of all American dance companies—that is to say, with its wide-ranging repertoire, it is the most similar in character and achievement to a European national company.

The second person is Lincoln Kirstein, who, like Diaghilev, is neither dancer, musician, nor painter: and when, in the early 1930's, he became intensely interested in ballet, he was no more than moderately wealthy. In Europe he found George Balanchine, a brilliant talent somewhat adrift after Diaghilev's death, and Kirstein straightaway decided to ignore doctors' predictions that Balanchine had only three years to live, believing instead that he had a destiny to fulfill for the ballet in America. They young choreographer in failing health is now the sprightly, prolific, seventy-five-year-old director of the New York City Ballet, and perceptive Kirstein is its "éminence grise." Over the years he has nurtured Balanchine's remarkable creativity, always leaving him total artistic freedom to mould, in his own way, the new classical dance style that links his Russian inheritance with the athleticism and buoyancy of cool American youth. That is how new traditions are evolved.

It would be rather absurd to write so much about dance without mentioning music; the two are so interlinked that for a ballet to be successful it should have music that at the very least is appropriate to its subject and the period of its presentation, as was true of the court entertainments composed expressly for each occasion by the best available musicians. A particularly important celebration staged by Balthasar de Beaujoyeulx in 1573 included a scene of sixteen ladies of the court dancing a series of complicated patterns to the sound of thirty violins—and a very pretty effect it must have been.

Since ballet masters were also musicians and poets, and since royal princes were also dancers, if not choreographers and composers as well; there was little division between the arts and no discrimination; therefore ballet began its life supported by the finest musical inspiration. Louis XIV's official composer, Lully, had the advantage of being an expert dancer, so everything went well under his direction until he grew too old to keep abreast of the times. Then professional dancers acquired bad habits, insisting that their favourite

JEAN BAPTISTE LULLY

JEAN-PHILIPPE RAMEAU

pieces be interpolated into new works regardless of musical coherence. Ballet masters, too, began to believe that music existed to serve their steps instead of the other way around. Things went from bad to worse, causing Noverre, late in the eighteenth century, to say that ballet at the Opera was "a spectacle fit for monkeys."

There were noble exceptions. Jean-Philippe Rameau, born in 1683, wrote many good ballet-operas; he understood the medium perfectly. Handel wrote a ballet prologue especially for Marie Sallé in 1734, Gluck composed several ballets for the Italian choreographer Angiolini in Vienna during the 1760's, and Beethoven wrote two ballets, of which *Creatures of Prometheus,* given in 1801, also in Vienna, is the better known; the choreographer was Salvatore Viganò. Both he, from Naples, and Angiolini, from Florence, were the sons of dancers and composed music themselves (Viganò was the nephew of the composer Boccherini). In 1778 Mozart wrote *Les Petits Riens* for Noverre in Paris.

During the nineteenth century even the best ballet masters remained unadventurous regarding music. They frankly didn't believe that any but the most straightforward rhythms and uncomplicated pieces were danceable, and these, for the most part, were supplied by a house composer attached to the theatre, perhaps as a member of the orchestra. Ferdinand Hérold was one who composed a number of ballets while he was a répétiteur at the Opera,

LÉO DELIBES

including the 1826 version of *La Fille Mal Gardée* and an early, forgotten *Sleeping Beauty*.

The most successful, and undoubtedly most prolific, house composer was an Italian, Cesare Pugni, with three hundred and twelve ballets to his credit, all of them—if the surviving and, presumably, best are anything to judge by—distinctly "pretty-pretty." But he did write expressly for ballet, whereas better composers were not much interested, except when dancing scores were called for in their operas. This was a contractual stipulation in Paris, where the last act of every opera had to start with a ballet because of a custom instituted by Dr. Véron, the director who had cleverly played Elssler off against Taglioni. He had opened the behind-the-scenes Foyer de la Danse to selected ticket holders so that they could dally there with the girls during the intermission, and it became a requisite for any man who wanted to be in the swim of Parisian society to attend the Foyer and, preferably, to choose his mistress from among the dancers. Thus Dr. Véron made his theatre the hub of fashion, attracting alike music-lovers and those with an ear like a boot, and it is he we must thank for the bulk of good opera-ballet music, including some Verdi and Rossini added especially for their Paris productions.

A later Opera director, bent on moral reform, abolished entry to the Foyer de la Danse and tried to segregate the sexes backstage by installing separate staircases—though heaven knows what pranks he imagined might take place on the stairs. Under his direction

PETER ILYICH TCHAIKOVSKY

the theatre nearly went bankrupt so he was hastily replaced; the Foyer was reopened and all prospered again as before.

The situation between choreographer and musician is best illustrated by Tchaikovsky, who remains always the giant among ballet composers. In 1875 the director of the Bolshoi Theatre in Moscow commissioned Tchaikovsky—for a fee equivalent to $400, which he needed because his generosity left him constantly short of funds—to write a full-evening ballet called *Swan Lake*. Tchaikovsky accepted readily, having long been attracted by the challenge of this branch of theatre composition, although he was sure he could never equal Delibes' *Coppélia* of 1870.

Swan Lake was presented in Moscow the same year as Delibes' next ballet, *Sylvia*, and Tchaikovsky wrote: "*Swan Lake* is poor stuff in comparison." What an idea! It is the most beautiful, satisfying, and enduring music ever written for a full-evening ballet. Nevertheless, the inept choreographer of this unsuccessful production—a nonentity named Reisinger—found some sections so difficult that he replaced them with familiar bits from other works, a common practice that shocked no one then since it was normal for two or three composers to share responsibility for a new ballet. Naturally, such scores were derided by serious musicians, and when Tchaikovsky's Fourth Symphony was completed, an ex-pupil whose opinion he valued complained that many phrases "sounded like ballet music," which spoiled his enjoyment of the rest. In defense, Tchaikovsky replied:

> *I have no idea what you consider ballet music or why you should object to it. Do you look upon every melody in a lively dance rhythm as "ballet music?" If so, how do you reconcile yourself to most of Beethoven's symphonies, in which you will find such melodies on every page? Or do you intend to say that the trio of my Scherzo is in the style of Minkus, Gerber, or Pugni? To my mind, it does not deserve such criticism. I can never understand why "ballet music" should be used as an epithet of contempt. The music of ballet is not invariably bad, for there are good works of this class—Delibes' Sylvia, for example. And when the music is good, what difference does it make whether Sobyesichanskaya dances to it or not? I can only think that certain parts of my symphony displease you because they recall the ballet, not because they are intrinsically bad.*

The Sleeping Beauty was commissioned in 1889 by Vsevolojsky, the director of the Maryinsky Theatre in St. Petersburg, for Marius Petipa to choreograph. As he did for every composer, Petipa gave Tchaikovsky a detailed summary of the type of music and length of each piece he wanted. It was twelve years after the *Swan Lake* failure in Moscow for which

Tchaikovsky unjustifiably always blamed his music, and he was keen to do better with his second ballet. Before coming to Act III, he took the trouble to study the score of Adolphe Adam's *Giselle* diligently. What higher tribute could any ballet score receive? And who should be surprised that *Giselle* has lasted so well these one hundred and forty-odd years? Tchaikovsky appreciated how perfectly apt its music was for its purpose.

When Petipa choreographed *The Sleeping Beauty,* he didn't find it easy. He was accustomed to "ballet music" and had been satisfied with Ludwig Minkus, a house composer in Russia for many years, whose best-known ballet now is *Don Quixote.* Tchaikovsky's music, even composed to measure, was very different; he was a symphonist, and the scale of his writing, conceiving the ballet as one complete work rather than a series of items strung together, had symphonic size. In the orchestration he created several entirely new effects which, as he explained to a friend, he hoped would be "both interesting and useful."

Not only were Petipa and the dancers put to the test by this innovative "ballet music," but so also was the public, and Tchaikovsky wrote in his diary that the Czar's only comment was " 'Very charming.' His Majesty treated me in the most off-hand manner. God be with him." How hard it is now to grasp that people could have been bewildered by the novelty of this music! It is so clear and so expressive of the action at every point; every emotion is there, waiting only to be danced in the spirit in which it was composed— and, for that, the dancer has only to hear with the heart.

One feels that Tchaikovsky understood dance through and through. The fact that he knew nothing of its steps mattered not in the least; he was totally in sympathy with the rhythms and emotions of dance. I think this affinity was simply that, emotionally, he lived at a matching pace. He was so highly strung, complex, self-critical, shy, impatient, and anguished, that a short, quick variation for a dancer was also an accurate expression of his own nervousness; the two shared a common tempo. His passionate love of the Russian countryside and longing for it when he was away could also be read into his long, melodic passages tinged with nostalgia, and the reassuring waltzes reflect his joy in full-blown, peaceful summer days. The deeper suffering of his emotional life comes out in darker, dramatic passages. Experiencing a performance of one of his works is like living a microcosm of his life. He had a truly Russian soul.

Music, supposedly, affects only one of the five senses, but could there not be a sixth sense associated with physical response? Instead of "tangible" or "visible," could there not be "danceable"? Anyway, it is a fact that Tchaikovsky's ballets are supremely so.

With Tchaikovsky, ballet began to regain some standing as a theatre art, and the story continues in Russian hands with Glazunov's *Raymonda* and *The Seasons,* and then Stravinsky's magnificent *The Firebird, Petrouchka,* and *The Rite of Spring.* Only with those works did choreographers, namely, Fokine and Nijinsky, discard all the restrictions of orthodox steps and abandon themselves to follow unknown musical territory. They and the dancers found it as difficult as traversing a thick forest without a compass. An immensely important aspect of Diaghilev's revolution was that he wrenched ballet out of its lazy ways in a musical backwater. The less good part was that he made one-act ballets so important that two- or three-act works came to appear hopelessly old-fashioned. Now that they have returned to favour with the public, there seem to be few composers willing to write them. Thanks to Russia we have Prokofiev's *Romeo and Juliet* and *Cinderella;* other Soviet works there are too, but not so outstanding. Stravinsky unfortunately never composed a long ballet. Around Europe there have been isolated cases of important scores commissioned for full-scale ballets, although more consistently it is the smaller companies and modern dance groups that are thinking in terms of contemporary music.

It is very difficult to find composers eager and able to write good ballets, but I think over-dependence on concert scores is dangerous. Remembering back to the founding of ballet, when it went hand in hand with music, it would be tragic to allow the two to stray apart again; tragic, that is, for ballet. But that is just what is happening.

DANCE TRADITIONAL

At about the same time that women dancers first appeared at the Paris Opera, in 1681, a Mr. Dick Sadler, in the green countryside north of London, opened a modest Musick House at his home where music and song entertained patrons from the neighbouring areas. One day workmen digging in his garden came across some ancient covered-over wells. From that simple discovery the name Sadler's Wells was born, and it has been associated with a place of entertainment on the same site for nearly three hundred years.

The well waters were full of minerals which gave a steely tang. When eminent physicians began recommending them to cure anything and everything from scurvy to "Virgin's Fever"—whatever that was—people suddenly flocked out to Sadler's Wells, hundreds at a time, by carriage, on horseback, and on foot. They were advised to drink the water in the early morning and at intervals throughout the day, taking mild exercise in between. With business booming, Mr. Sadler was able to lay out attractive gardens where visitors could stroll by the river bordering his property. He also built a larger entertainment room.

After a while, like all health fads, the waters went out of fashion and Mr. Sadler fell back on his original enterprise, which was to lure as many people as possible from the crowded city during the summer months for some fresh air and light amusement. As the years went by, and the place passed through the hands of different owners, with the usual ups and downs of the theatre business, the types of entertainment varied considerably. For a time drink and bawdy songs brought in a very rough clientele; sometimes they were offered bizarre acts like the "Hibernian Cannibal," who ate live chickens without the aid of a knife or fork but washed down with a pint of brandy.

When a proper theatre was built, high-class pantomime and spectacle greatly improved the tone. Serious drama was ruled out because two London theatres alone held the necessary patents, or licenses. Their monopoly forced other managements into all kinds of subterfuge; pantomime, clowning, singing, amazing scenic transformations, and the like.

SADLER'S WELLS THEATRE, 1792

At Sadler's Wells one of the many attractions that made the theatre famous was a water tank, three feet deep, set in the stage for the reproduction, in very realistic fashion, of great sea battles. An Australian theatre proprietor copied some of the novelties of Melbourne, including a front curtain made entirely of small mirrors. In decline, the "Wells" served as a boxing arena and fell into neglect until rebuilt in its present form in 1931.

Of all the people who brought laughter and tears to the old Sadler's Wells, the greatest, and the one who most delights the imagination, was Joseph Grimaldi, known as a clown but who was much more than that—a dancer, a mime, an acrobat, and a comic genius. He extended the English development of commedia dell'arte and harlequinade, of satire and fooling, and of absurd invention that was inherited by all subsequent clowns down to Little Tich—whom Nijinsky admired passionately—and Charlie Chaplin, not forgetting Laurel and Hardy. Grimaldi's face and India-rubber body were a miracle of expression that conveyed everything ludicrous, inspired, joyful, or pathetic in the human

SADLER'S WELLS AQUATIC THEATRE, 1800

character; and an endless range of new tricks sprang continuously from his imagination. His sense of fun was overwhelmingly infectious, but when he commiserated with an oyster crossed in love the whole house was in tears.

Grimaldi's body, "without any bone in it and, apparently, without any centre of gravity," was inherited from dancing parents. His Italian father, who was sixty-two when Joe was born, came from Italy in the 1750's as a dentist appointed to the queen; but he far preferred his second profession as dancer, so he abandoned the grim occupation of tooth-pulling in favour of the London stage, and was ballet master at Drury Lane till the end of his life. His strength and spectacular leaps brought him the nickname "Iron-Legs."

Such an old father might easily have spoiled his son, but not Iron-Legs. Instead he thrashed him frequently for his high spirits. In spite of this, Joe was irrepressible and remained the embodiment of ebullience throughout his career of forty-four hard years that began at Sadler's Wells in 1784, when he was three years old. His father, still strong and

JOSEPH GRIMALDI

active, was playing the summer season: he took Joe on stage with him in *Robinson Crusoe* dressed as a monkey on a chain. He was an instant success. One night, as his father swung him round in the air, the chain broke, sending Joe flying over the orchestra to land in the arms of a very surprised gentleman in the stalls. Joe was so small and light that neither of them was hurt. Another time, wearing an ill-fitting cat mask, he failed to see an open trap and fell forty feet, escaping with no more than a broken collarbone and some bruises.

His father soon had him engaged to play Sadler's Wells and Drury Lane simultaneously, which meant walking back and forth between the two by day to rehearse, and running from one to the other at night to fulfill both performances, each one enough to exhaust a working man. He kept up and increased this pace in maturity. It was normal for him to make twenty costume changes in one pantomime and his exuberance never flagged. No wonder he was too crippled before he was fifty to carry on any longer. Surely no one ever made a more touching farewell speech than this:

GRIMALDI AT HIS DEBUT AND FAREWELL PERFORMANCES

Ladies and Gentlemen,

I appear before you for the last time. I need not assure you of the sad regret with which I say it; but sickness and infirmity have come upon me, and I can no longer wear the motley! Four years ago I jumped my last jump, filched my last custard, and ate my last sausage. I cannot describe the pleasure I felt on once more assuming my cap and bells tonight—that dress in which I have so often been made happy in your applause; and as I stripped them off, I fancied that they seemed to cleave to me. I am not so rich a man as I was when I was basking in your favour formerly, for then I had always a fowl in one pocket and sauce for it in the other. [Laughter and applause from the audience.] I thank you for the benevolence which has brought you here to assist your old and faithful servant in his premature decline. Eight-and-forty years have not yet passed over my head, and I am sinking fast. I now stand worse on my legs than I used to do on my head. But I suppose I am paying the penalty for the cause I pursued all my

AS A CLOWN   AS HOCK

IN *ALL THE WORLD'S IN PARIS*

KING HUMMING TOP OR HARLEQUIN AND THE LAND OF TOYS, DRURY LANE THEATRE, 1853

life; my desire and anxiety to merit your favour has excited me to more exertion than my constitution would bear; and, like vaulting ambition, I have overleaped myself. Ladies and Gentlemen, I must hasten to bid you farewell; but the pain I feel in doing so is assuaged by seeing before me a disproof of the old adage that favourites have no friends. Ladies and Gentlemen, may you and yours ever enjoy the blessings of health is the fervent prayer of Joseph Grimaldi—Farewell! Farewell!

As he spoke he was sitting on a chair. It was at Drury Lane Theatre in June 1828.

Offstage he was a quiet, simple, generous man who well knew the proverbial heart-break behind the clown's greasepaint. He outlived his devoted wife, his brilliant but drunkard son, and a younger brother, who vanished without trace the very night he returned from fourteen years at sea. Joe was overwhelmed with emotion at rediscovering the long-lost sailor only to lose him again immediately to the London street thugs who almost certainly murdered him for his seafarer's fortune.

A few months before Joe died, living alone and unable to walk, but accepting his fate philosophically, he completed writing his memoirs with this little epitaph:

Life is a game we are bound to play,
The wise enjoy it, fools grow sick of it,
Losers, we find, have the stakes to pay,
        That winners may laugh, for that's the trick of it.

Perhaps Grimaldi would not be so important to this story if Britain had had a state or royal ballet in the eighteenth century like so many cities in the rest of Europe. The best elements in dance would have been channelled into the royal company; Grimaldi himself might have become a great character dancer instead of a superb clown. Who knows?

Since there was no such stable, subsidized organization until after World War II, the whole history of dance in Britain was one of individual and commercial enterprise. It had to please a wide public or fail. But the British respond better to a challenge than an easy situation, and the result has been the special virtue of our British choreographers—namely, to use dance dramatically rather than for its own sake. The elements of acting and story-telling are stronger than the making of pure dance patterns, while wit, and humour, are never far away.

The inherited tradition of British dance comes from the theatre as well as the ballet

RICHARD FLEXMORE (1824–60),
CLOWN AND DANCER

FREDERICK ASHTON AND ROBERT HELPMANN
IN *CINDERELLA*, 1965

studio; it comes from Shakespeare, Garrick, and Grimaldi, blended with Perrot, Petipa, and Fokine. The Grimaldi inheritance is very old, deriving from the Greek and Roman art of acting without words. The Roman performers Pylades and Bathyllus, living under Caesar Augustus in the first years of Christendom, were called pantomimes, not actors or dancers. They were so popular that fans fought heatedly and publicly over which was the greater performer. As this form of dumb-show filtered through the centuries it was associated with commedia dell'arte, and that led to harlequinade, which found tremendous favour in England, where it was eventually dissolved into that strange concoction called the Christmas Pantomime. Song and speech have found their way into it intermittently, but from the moment it took the British public's fancy, dancing was part and parcel of the charade—and comedy an absolute essential.

So comic dances are as natural to the British stage as the scenery, the footlights, and certain stock characters of the Christmas Pantomime—the Dame, always played by a man, the Principal Boy, played by a girl, and Buttons, the faithful page. The Ugly Sisters in Frederick Ashton's *Cinderella* or the half-wit suitor and scheming mother in his *Fille Mal Gardée* belong to British ballet as to no other, for no other country has anything quite resembling this living evolution of an ancient art with all its tricks and "business" augmented over many generations. This vitality of the commercial theatre was food for British ballet when it became, so belatedly, a national organization.

In 1758 a critic writing about Iron-Legs' first London appearance made the point that Italian dancers were better actors than the French, whom he dismissed, with their "graceful posturings," as obviously less interesting. Since the founding of ballet at the Paris Opera, and well before that when it was a court pastime, technique and style were all-important to the French. The few dancers who believed ballet could and should express deep emotions made little impact on the happy progress of pure dance. In London it was always different. Although the monarchs had usually enjoyed dancing and, in the sixteenth and seventeenth centuries, produced the particularly beautiful court ballets called masques, none of them was inclined to follow Louis XIV's example and establish professional dance (or any form of royal theatre for that matter). Therefore, in the theatre, it was never a nobleman's art but belonged to the populace, who liked a bit of action, especially some clowning. The upper classes never took dance seriously as an art, mainly because religious influences had too often through the ages damned it as a ruse of the Devil—and one must remember that the Devil and Hell were very real beliefs—so, although social dances were always fashionable, and nothing will stop young people from following the fashion, there was nevertheless a great deal of disapproval and even fear in many minds.

SCENE FROM COMMEDIA DELL'ARTE, C. 1580

Into this atmosphere was born one of the most important figures in the history of ballet, whose name, John Weaver, is almost unknown because there was no state ballet to blow a trumpet for him. By the time Britain's Royal Ballet received its royal title, Weaver had been dead and forgotten nearly two hundred years; and yet he was not only brilliant in many ways but one of the most charming and lovable of all ballet masters—also quite inexplicable as an Englishman. There had been very important Italian and French writers on dance and notation; all the significant progress had developed in those two countries until, one day in 1673, shortly after the Paris Opera was established and less than ten years before Mr. Sadler found his wells, John Weaver was born in the prosperous town of Shrewsbury. His father taught social dancing to the gentry, and John in turn became dancing master at Shrewsbury Grammar School, where he had received an excellent education, as one can tell by his erudite writings. He was by no means a dry, boring theoretician even though he wrote extraordinarily advanced books on dance, relating it to music (which was unusual) and to anatomy (which no one else had thought of), as well as putting it in historical perspective to counter current prejudices.

As a man, Weaver was full of vitality and charm, much loved and much loving. He had, probably, two wives and no one knows how many children, and enjoyed a drink as much as anyone. In Shrewsbury he was known with affection as a dapper, busy little man who was always cheerful and of generous heart.

When he was about twenty-five, he started going up to London, where he met the élite teachers of his day: Mr. Isaacs, Thomas Caverly—said to have lived to one hundred years—and Mr. Essex, who is pictured in William Hogarth's series called "The Rake's Progress," which inspired Ninette de Valois to create a classic English ballet in 1935. Weaver's sudden appearance from Shrewsbury, fully trained and extremely well read, might have surprised the capital if a prophet were ever recognized in his own country, but his contribution to dance over the next thirty-odd years was little understood—very likely he did not even appreciate it himself—and he returned from whence he came, cheerful as ever, to die in Shrewsbury in 1760 at the age of eighty-seven.

Weaver was deeply impressed by the English style of ballroom dancing as taught by the eminent London masters. It was easy, graceful, and unaffected, yet retained all the elegance of the more rigid French school. To promote these high standards around the country, he translated and published a French system of notation which brought order to dance teaching and respectability to the profession. In addition, he thoroughly understood professional ballet and saw what future possibilities it held when it advanced into drama. He said dancers must act out the emotions of the characters they portrayed; ballets must tell their stories without words; male and female dance movements were different in style and expression; ballet music must reflect the difference between danced or mimed passages; costumes should be historically accurate; and so on. All these ideas, which now seem so obvious, were revolutionary when Weaver put them into practice, although they had been floating about vaguely in some minds.

Weaver's first ballet based on these principles appeared in 1717. It was the first bal-

JEAN-GEORGES NOVERRE

let ever presented without using speech or song to tell the story; in his program Weaver apologized for the difficulty his dancers found working in so unaccustomed a manner ("I have not been able to get all my dancers equal to the design"). But he was fortunate to have the artistry of beautiful Mrs. Santlow for his ballerina and Dupré, from Paris, for her partner. He himself, a good character dancer as well as choreographer, teacher, and writer, played Vulcan. The ballet was called *The Loves of Mars and Venus* and was received at the Drury Lane Theatre with great enthusiasm.

At Lincoln's Inn Theatre, not far away, the ten-year-old Marie Sallé was also enjoying a great success dancing with her twelve-year-old brother. When she grew up, Marie Sallé returned often to London, where her own choreographic innovations, in the spirit of Weaver's ideals, were far more appreciated than in her native Paris. She was such an intelligent artist and fine dancer that she was able to spearhead the ballet reforms, still advancing rather slowly, twenty years after *The Loves of Mars and Venus.*

Louis Dupré was another who enjoyed working in London with Weaver and danced in many of his ballets. When he was much older he had a pupil in Paris called Jean-Georges Noverre, who managed to take upon himself the credit for almost everything that Weaver had done first and Sallé, among others, had developed, but for which they received little recognition.

ANDRÉ DESHAYES AND JAMES HARVEY D'EGVILLE IN *ARCHILLE ET DÉIDAMIE*

Noverre was a great choreographer but a rather mean man. He filched other people's ideas and published them as his own. His *Lettres sur la Danse*, published in 1760, the year Weaver died, was widely read in Europe and accepted as gospel for the kind of work called the ballet d'action, in which dance and drama combine, as opposed to divertissement ballets that consist of suites of dances on a theme, but without a story. Noverre is often credited with inventing the ballet d'action. The late Derra de Moroda, who was the best-informed dance historian on this period, wrote:

> *As Noverre explains his ideas in such a brilliant form in his* Lettres, *he does not leave one in doubt that all these ideas are his very own, and no one ever thought of these innovations before him—all other ballet masters of his time are either his pupils and disciples, or his imitators, who live on his ideas, which they have stolen from him seeing and copying his works.*
>
> *Now, let us see how far all this is true, but before we go any further let us state once and for all that the ballet d'action is not an invention but an evolution. . . .*

She then quotes several writers and choreographers who expounded similar principles prior to Noverre, and cites Weaver's *The Loves of Mars and Venus* as "what one could claim as the first real and complete ballet d'action."

CHARLES-LOUIS DIDELOT AND MLLE. THÉODORE IN *THE PROSPECT BEFORE US*, 1791

Noverre is a difficult character to assess, although there is no doubt everyone praised his enormous talent as a choreographer. I think the fact that he was never much of a dancer rankled all his life, making him touchy, at times bitter, and determined on a place in history by other means. When he was only about twenty-eight he received an offer from the illustrious English actor-manager David Garrick to stage his recent success, *Metamorphoses Chinoises,* at the Drury Lane Theatre. He refused the financial terms outright and stated his minimum demand, adding somewhat arrogantly, "This is my last word. Please be so good as to make up your mind because I do not wish to answer the proposal of the Bavarian Court before I know your latest intentions." (This reminds me of a French ballerina in the 1840's, whose ambitious mother so often announced magnificent contracts pouring in from foreign cities that the poor girl ended up with no offers at all as everyone thought she was fully booked up.)

Another cause of Noverre's intense frustration was that, in spite of the acclaim that greeted his productions at the Opéra Comique and wherever else he went, the Opera declined his application for the post of ballet master. Viewed historically, this seems to have been the greatest blunder they ever made, but in a way it was unavoidable, owing to the rule that each ballet master was succeeded by the senior leading dancer, who in his turn always held on to the position as long as he could. Noverre did not dance well enough to enter the Opera and go through these channels. Consequently, as a hot-headed young man with no modesty concerning his own talents, he was aggrieved that the Opera did not make way specially for his exciting productions, which they certainly needed. Always bearing this grudge, he went elsewhere to perfect his mastery of sensationally beautiful presentations, each more expensive than the last, and proclaim his own genius in his writings. When his naturally quick temper was encouraged by a few drinks, all his grievances came forth in violent language.

When he was fifty the Opera finally admitted his right, as the greatest master of his day, to become chief ballet master. From the moment he set foot in the place there was jealousy, suspicion, obstructionism, factionism, criticism, and every other difficulty imaginable. One cannot but sympathize deeply with him for this souring of his whole life's fulfillment. The young Queen Marie Antoinette, who had been his pupil as a child at the Viennese court, understood and valued his importance. She gave all the support in her power, including the promise of a royal pension, which unluckily, like her beautiful head, was cut off in the Revolution.

Noverre had resigned from the Opera in bitterness and gone to London, where rave reviews must have comforted him a little, even though many spectators in the pit could not see his ballets for the enormous bonnets of the ladies, and those able to see the stage could scarcely pick out the dancers from the throng of spectators milling about during the performance. Warnings that they might fall down traps did nothing to put them off. Nevertheless, everyone who was anyone danced at the King's Theatre at this time.

There were visits from captivating Mlle. Théodore, who so enjoyed London that she contrived, with Marie Antoinette's influence, to get her Opera contract annulled. The minute she returned to Paris for a day, the Opera retaliated by putting her in prison on the pretext that she had criticized the management. Dauberval followed her to London because he found her irresistible. They married later, and she was the first to dance Lise in *La Fille Mal Gardée*. Guimard—the Skeleton of the Graces—forever feminine and fascinating but no longer very young, came to London as a refugee from the Revolution. Her partner was Didelot, then aged twenty-two, who was to create "flying ballets" and find his life's mission moulding the ballet in Russia.

Then there was Charles Le Picq, the "Apollo of Dance," whose very walk was beyond all comparison. He also danced and choreographed in Russia for a while and gave some lessons to Count Sheremetiev's serfs. The younger Vestris danced in London with his father in 1781—Parliament interrupted its sessions to see them—and again after the French Revolution, when he stayed four years with Noverre. Antoine Bournonville, whose son would become the genius of Danish ballet, was there, and so too was young Coulon, who much later would have a little pupil named Marie Taglioni.

In 1789 the King's Theatre burned down, leading to a ridiculous battle between its brilliant and dogged manager, Mr. Taylor, and an upstart rival named Mr. O'Reilly, who quickly took up the license for opera and ballet and opened at the Pantheon Theatre with all of Mr. Taylor's stars. He had Mlle. Théodore, Dauberval, and Didelot, and added for good measure the very artistic couple Salvatore Viganò and his wife, Maria Medina, who was so like an early Isadora Duncan. Mr. Taylor, furious, rented the Little Theatre and weighed in with both the Vestrises, father and son, among his box-office attractions. Mr. O'Reilly, claiming he held the exclusive license, tried to have them all arrested. Mr. Taylor avoided that blow, but succumbed financially to the competition and had to close. Mr. O'Reilly's gloating tempted the fates: his Pantheon Theatre burned to a cinder and Mr. Taylor triumphantly scooped up the dancers in time to open his re-built King's Theatre with a scintillating new Noverre production. In 1940 Ninette de Valois made a ballet on this farcical story, *The Prospect Before Us*, in which Robert Helpmann created one of his greatest comedy characterizations as Mr. O'Reilly, who philosophically drowned his sorrows in an unforgettable drunken dance when all was lost.

The English pantomimes did not impress Noverre one bit. As a man of cultural sensitivity, he found them tawdry and unsubtle. Yet he was full of admiration for their by-product in the form of scenic engineering. London theatres excelled in machinery for instantaneous transformations in a hundred varieties, and any illusion he desired could be realized to his total satisfaction; the commercial theatre knew its business well.

Alas that so much of this magic craft has been forgotten and the simplest effects these days seem fraught! Without *Peter Pan* and the Christmas pantomimes, it is doubtful that anyone would maintain the technique, so ingeniously exploited by Didelot, of flying people on wires—a technique he used first in London. It was not a feature of Bournonville's creations in Copenhagen, where many of the other tricks and machines have remained in constant use to remind us of charms long since vanished elsewhere.

The fortunes of British ballet rested in the hands of independent theatrical managers. The financial hazards of presenting opera and ballet—for they always shared the bill—led almost inevitably to bankruptcy, so one must salute the brave men who plied London with all that was best in continental dance, in particular the discerning Mr. Lumley, who took over Her Majesty's Theatre in 1842 and straightaway engaged Jules Perrot as his ballet master for a series of seasons that brought every important dancer to London—some before Paris even saw them. Britain is therefore not lacking in dance history; the difficulty was to build any kind of a national standard. Employment on a seasonal basis did not admit of a strong corps de ballet from which stars could emerge. Without a permanent school and proving ground the native dancers were always at a disadvantage.

The same situation often prevailed in European courts, where patronage was a matter of each prince's whim. Those who were clever found good ballet masters to build important centres of creation—Stuttgart became one while Noverre was there—only to have them decline under successors who were uninterested. As Grimaldi said, "That's the trick of it."

In the end, everything comes down to a question of individuals. For example, in the 1880's, when London opera-goers had lost interest in the artificialities of opera-ballet and sent it packing to the music hall, two theatres, the Alhambra and the Empire, achieved remarkably high standards within their limitations. And here an important point in the story is reached. A ballet mistress, Katti Lanner at the Empire, enters for the first time after such a long succession of gentlemen have monopolized the creative side of dance.

KATTI LANNER

Since there was no longer any esteem for men on the stage and, correspondingly, little inducement for them to involve themselves at all in the business of ballet, it was inevitable that their place should sometimes be taken by women as performers, directors, and choreographers. As such, Katti Lanner was the first link in a chain of female names that leads directly to the founding of British national ballet. She spanned a transitional period between Romantic ballet and the Isadora Duncan wave of feminism. In 1829, when Katti was born in Vienna, Auguste Vestris had not long given up dancing to become the most sought-after teacher in Paris, Marie Taglioni had not yet danced *La Sylphide* (it came three years later), and Marius Petipa was eleven years old. At sixteen Katti made her début in the Kärntnertor Theatre, where a fellow Viennese, Fanny Elssler, had made her first appearance and was soon to give her farewell season.

Apart from her considerable dancing career in Europe and America, it is possible that Katti was the first important woman choreographer. Ten ballets for Hamburg by the time she was thirty-three were only a start. When she went to the Empire she was fifty-eight, with a lifetime of theatre experience behind her, so the management could hardly have made a better choice. In all, she created thirty-three ballets there, with a large company well disciplined under her autocratic rule. Leading ballerinas, including Carlotta Brianza, whom Petipa chose for his first Princess Aurora in *The Sleeping Beauty*, considered it a prestigious engagement. And Pierina Legnani displayed her sensational thirty-two fouetté turns at the Alhambra in London before Petipa put them into *Swan Lake* for her.

We certainly would find Katti's choreography inanely unsophisticated; so were a lot of the more serious efforts being presented all over Europe. It was not a very sophisticated world. But one can imagine that her work was ideal for the time and place or she would not have remained ten years in a highly competitive theatre. Besides, as the daughter of the waltz composer Joseph Lanner, she had an excellent musical pedigree, and the resident musical director had an unusual flair for the needs of dance. Between them, I feel sure they did a very splendid job.

In Katti Lanner's last year at the Empire a new guest ballerina arrived who was quite different from all the others. Neither Italian nor French, nor strong, efficient, or somehow earthy like her predecessors, she was a trim, fair-haired, unspoiled nineteen-year-old from Copenhagen. Her name, Adeline Genée, meant nothing, but she had the assurance of four or five years of engagements in the Berlin and Munich court theatres, and her dancing was exceptionally fluent. Her parents had handed her over completely in her early childhood to an aunt and a ballet master uncle. She was obedient, hard-working, and so talented that he was able to make her into a matchless dancer as light and brilliant as a hummingbird.

Having arrived in London in 1897 with a contract for six weeks, she stayed ten years, by which time there was scarcely a mouse that had not heard of Genée at the Empire. Thousands of ordinary folk who would never have gone to an opera house fell under her spell. It was not ballet they went to see—most of them cared not a fig for dance—but Genée was another matter. She was enchantment.

An amusing essay written by Max Beerbohm in 1906 begins by saying that, as a writer, ballet has no meaning for him because where there are no words is a void. Then he complains of a disproportion between a ballerina's arms and her muscular legs: "It is natural enough that a woman should dance sometimes just as it is natural that she should walk, sit, lie down. But it is unnatural that dancing should be the business of her life. And nature takes vengeance by destroying her symmetry, by making her ridiculous. Poor ballerina!" He turns to Mlle. Genée and says:

Ah no; I grant an exception there. . . . A mermaid were not a more surprising creature than she—she of whom one half is as that of an authentic ballerina, whilst the other is that of a most intelligent, most delightfully human actress. A mermaid were indeed less marvellous in our eyes. She would not be able to defuse any semblance of humanity into her tail. Mlle. Genée's intelligence seems to vibrate to her very toes. Her dancing, strictliest classical though it is, is a part of her acting. And her acting, moreover, is of so fine a quality that she makes the old ineloquent conventions of gesture tell their meanings to me, and tell them so exquisitely that I quite forget my craving for words.

ADELINE GENÉE

She was a soubrette ballerina, with an effervescent personality. To have become the queen of London's theatre in music-hall ballet was, nevertheless, no mean feat, since she enjoyed none of the trappings and considerations found in opera houses. She danced every night without fail, taking over the stage from comedians, conjurers, acrobats, performing dogs, and the lot. It was popular theatre with a popular public to which she gave a golden touch that must have caught many a philistine surprised to find himself really enjoying that "operatic dancing stuff."

GENÉE IN THE DIVERTISSEMENT FROM *ROBERT LE DIABLE*, 1909

Genée was a major addition to the British dance heritage. Her presence was an inestimable help to native talents. She was not considered a foreigner; she married an Englishman, belonged to England, held the friendship of the royal family, and gave all her years in retirement to fostering British ballet—the fact that she danced in Leicester Square, not Covent Garden, had an unsuspected significance: it meant that the force of genuinely British tradition was moving slowly towards its own national ballet. The opera houses had always been showcases for continental artists; the Empire was British through and through.

LILIAN BAYLIS   NINETTE DE VALOIS

Two disconnected events in 1898 were to result in the final move towards a permanent British company. In that year an excellent Victorian lady put the management of her south London theatre into the hands of her niece, Lilian Baylis; and in Ireland a girl was born who would take the stage name Ninette de Valois. Exactly thirty years later, Miss Baylis asked Miss de Valois to choreograph a short ballet at her theatre, the Old Vic in Waterloo Road. The ballet was Mozart's *Les Petits Riens,* and in time, those "little nothings" led to very great things, for they began Ninette de Valois' directorship of the Vic-Wells Ballet, which became in turn Sadler's Wells Ballet, and finally the Royal Ballet.

Since we are talking now of the twentieth century, it was no rich prince who said, "Let there be ballet." Lilian Baylis was a woman whose only riches were the theatre inherited from her aunt, and an awe-inspiring belief that the Good Lord, who wished her to provide the highest in theatre art for the lowliest of His flock, would provide the wherewithal—and so He did. With no dignified opera house at her disposal, no expensive foreign artists, nor any of the prerequisites for first-class opera and drama, she ended up by accomplishing what none before her had been able to do. After Baylis, London had its first English Opera, National Theatre, and Royal Ballet. How did she do it? By faith, integrity, and singleness of purpose. At the time of her death in 1937, only the foundations existed—others have carried out the construction—but how long might that have taken without her? And who else would have given Ninette de Valois her opportunity at exactly the

ASHTON WITH MARIE RAMBERT IN *A TRAGEDY OF FASHION*, LYDIA LOPOKOVA IN THE TANGO

moment when she was young enough to face the long uphill struggle, wise enough to know what had to be done, and old enough to have the authority to do it?

In 1928 Lilian Baylis had two companies, drama and opera, in the same theatre. That is a luxury possible only with a subsidy to help pay two groups of artists to perform half a week each. If they were all to act and sing every night she needed a second theatre. Derelict Sadler's Wells was waiting for her. She was not the person to be put off by a trifle such as having no money to buy and re-build. She knew it had to be done.

A public subscription was opened (Winston Churchill was among the sponsors), the plans were drawn up, the work put in hand, and Sadler's Wells was re-born in 1931, with a heavy building debt. Opera evenings soon extended to separate opera and ballet evenings—again two companies sharing one theatre, and the building debt not cleared. But when you have faith, and it has brought you Ninette de Valois, Frederick Ashton, and Alicia Markova, you just continue with faith. In the early part of this century, ballet companies could be made that way. Now it requires money as well. Inflation affects everything except the number of seats in a theatre, and there is a limit to the amount any one person can pay for a ticket. Inevitably comes the day when that amount no longer covers its proportion of the performance cost. That is the sad story of theatre today.

One reason the Vic-Wells Ballet took off so rapidly once the fuse had been lit by Baylis and de Valois was the exceptional group of people who had been gathering for some time and who were ready to help it blaze. Anna Pavlova died in 1931, but one could say she was the first snowdrop of spring from the day she chose England for her permanent home in 1912. She must have sensed the difference between Paris (where dance lived preciously in the royally founded Opera) and London (where it had always belonged to the popular theatre). Pavlova wanted to reach the largest possible public. She took many English girls into her company, finding them surprisingly well trained, thanks to the Empire and Alhambra ballets.

The next prize for England was Tamara Karsavina, who married a British diplomat in Russia and escaped the 1917 Revolution with him. London gained the benefit of her unique artistry as she encouraged and graced every early move the company made.

Diaghilev chose London to present his spectacular *Sleeping Princess* in 1921; financially it was a failure, but how many must have seen it in a run of three months at the Alhambra? And imagine how much that enriched the local dance world!

One of his ballerinas in that production, the diminutive and bubbling Lydia Lopokova, married the economist Maynard Keynes—that was a double scoring! Then there was Polish-born Marie Rambert, another diminutive dynamo with quicksilver wits. She was first smitten by Isadora Duncan, then took up ballet rather late after working with Nijinsky, then married an Englishman and directed her tiny Ballet Club in London in a crazily stimulating fever of energy. She is not comparable to any other director except, in a far-fetched metaphor, to Diaghilev, because of her gift for fostering in others the talents she did not exercise herself. As she was never a choreographer and danced very little, she had an overflow of vitality which is still unexhausted at ninety-one, and her mind is as perceptive as ever it was.

The young British ballet had no system for seeking out and training its talent. It depended on those who sought out the dance for themselves; consequently they were all very individual artists. A young Irishman adopted the stage name (everyone took a stage name then) of Anton Dolin, and might have been transformed by Diaghilev into a choreographer if he had not been so Irish and independent. His was the glossy aspect of stardom. His partner, Alicia Markova, was so extraordinary that Diaghilev engaged her as a slip of a fourteen-year-old. His death in 1929 deprived her of the setting she merited, so she returned to illuminate the Ballet Club and Sadler's Wells like a thousand-lustred chandelier among the rest of us little flickering candles.

From Australia came a born actor, Robert Helpmann. Seeing Pavlova in Sydney had opened the world of dance expression to him, and it was to Sadler's Wells that he ap-

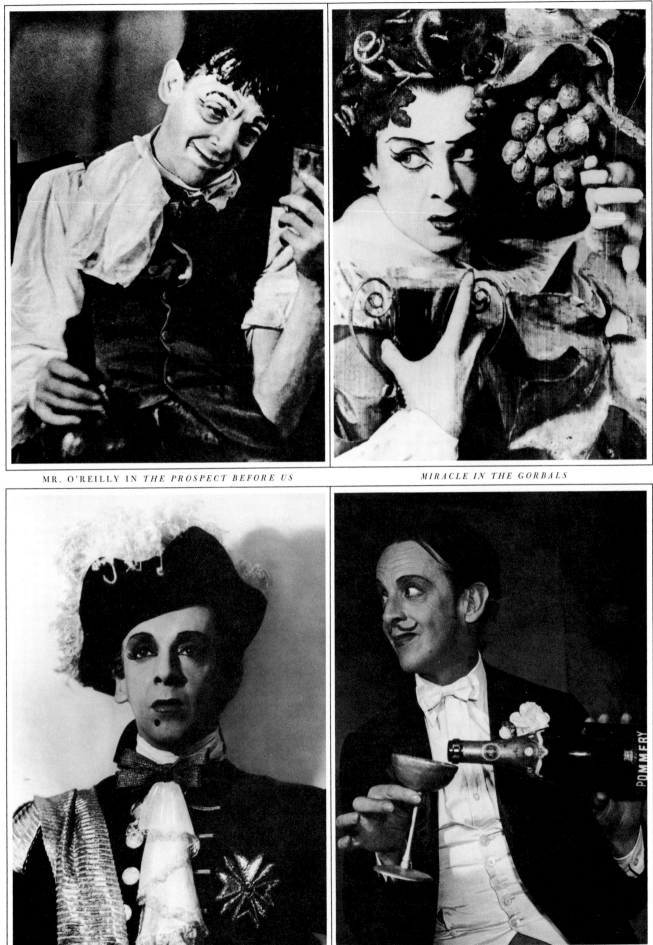

MR. O'REILLY IN *THE PROSPECT BEFORE US*   *MIRACLE IN THE GORBALS*

THE SLEEPING BEAUTY   *A WEDDING BOUQUET*

ANTON DOLIN IN *GISELLE*

ALICIA MARKOVA IN *GISELLE*

plied first on arriving in England. De Valois recognized a potential star at once. He was the rarest of all theatrical phenomena, the clown who could play Hamlet—which he did admirably both in Shakespeare and in a ballet of his own creating. One can imagine Grimaldi's spirit in the wings of his beloved Sadler's Wells Theatre observing Helpmann with a paternally approving smile. How alike they must have been as children! Slender, quick, and irrepressible, without a bone in their bodies, with india-rubber faces, and theatre sense in their veins. Helpmann has all the accumulated tradition of pantomime and harlequinade; the fine line between dance and acting gesture becomes invisible just as the fine line between comedy and pathos dissolves into the eternal truths of human nature. Ninette de Valois wrote of his interpretation of the toy-maker in *Coppélia*:

> *Great clowns are rare and Helpmann clowned Dr. Coppélius with genius—sharply outlining the old man's stupefying senility with nonsensical detail. He laid bare those flashes of guile shown by wicked old men who call on their wiles to offset their loneliness in a world they have set against themselves.*

Ninette de Valois herself I see as a very eighteenth-century artist, a direct descendant, both intellectually and creatively, of John Weaver, with his academic mind and thoroughgoing zest for work. Her priorities are not the modern ones of money and comfort, for which she does not give a damn, but people, achievement, knowledge, and the sense of humour that overrides life's vicissitudes. She is committed to the progress of dance, always questioning further, looking forward, gaining perspectives, placing each development in relation to the balance of the whole and re-assessing. Above all, she has that eighteenth-century gift of enthusiasm which will never leave her. In her eighty-first year she is still the most stimulating person in the world with whom to discuss dance.

Since it was she who made the national company and school, they did not exist to serve her when she was a student. She learned her craft with a touring children's troupe and in Christmas pantomimes; her art she learned with the Diaghilev ballet. Both were hard schools of the sink-or-swim category. The working conditions—long rehearsals, lack of rest, and lack of consideration—would never be tolerated by dancers today. But it was this experience that taught her what must be done in Britain. The Diaghilev ballet was mostly a homeless group of Russian expatriates whose dancing could not have held up indefinitely under such rough conditions without their strong technique gained in the Imperial schools. Having acquired her own training haphazardly by trial and error, she knew that she had to found a national school to feed a national company or native talents would

MARKOVA AND IGOR YOUSKEVITCH IN *ROUGE ET NOIR*

never have a chance to develop fully.

Markova's career was an example of the difficulties faced by talent without a national tradition to support it. When Diaghilev died, she was nineteen, one of the group whose precarious security lay in their orbit around his leadership. After his death they fell away in all directions like an upset bag of marbles, coming to rest wherever they could find some suitable opportunity to work. Markova returned to lead the budding British ballet.

With her tiny, slender figure, large dark eyes, and black hair, she was the picture of a ballerina. Fragile, quick, and light, she darted about the stage like a dragonfly, precise yet without effort or weight. No dancer has been so ethereal until Natalia Makarova, who now holds the place, in my estimation, that Markova held in my youth—that place being the summit to which all young ballerinas should aspire. Markova was invaluable to the young ballet in England, but the young English ballet was inadequate for her, not in repertoire, which suited her marvellously, but in importance. She was international; Sadler's Wells Ballet was local. She had to spread her wings and go to the sophisticated, colourful Ballet Russe, where her delicacy and elegance were framed in splendour.

NORA KAYE AND ANTONY TUDOR IN *PILLAR OF FIRE*

Somewhere in the early years I came into the English ballet. I was fourteen, with a minimum of concentrated training such as is mandatory now. I was nurtured, coaxed, coached, pushed, shouted at, nervous, in tears, cheerful, despairing, exhausted, exalted, and all the things in turn that go to making an artist. It took a long time. I was lucky to be reared in a company young enough and small enough to be a nursery.

As I grew up I was a part of the British ballet development. The most astonishing feature of its progress was the appearance of choreographers from nowhere. Throughout this story the ballet master sons of ballet masters reared on the language of dance gently advanced their inherited art. In England things happened differently. In 1931 an accountant named Antony Tudor suddenly took up dancing—out of office hours—at the age of twenty, and became a very distinctive choreographer, using simple ballet steps to reveal disquietingly complex psychological tensions. He was so original that others are still discovering the discoveries he made forty years ago. When he moved to New York he found Nora Kaye, an intensely dramatic ballerina, and his perfect interpreter of murky passions.

Left: RIO GRANDE WITH WALTER GORE, BEATRICE APPLEYARD, MARGOT FONTEYN, AND WILLIAM CHAPPEL
Right: LES PATINEURS WITH PAMELA MAY, MARGOT FONTEYN, AND JUNE BRAE

APPARITIONS WITH FONTEYN AND HELPMANN

ASHTON'S *THE DREAM* WITH ANTOINETTE SIBLEY AND ANTHONY DOWELL; AND *A MONTH IN THE COUNTRY* WITH DENISE NUNN, ALEXANDER GRANT, LYNN SEYMOUR, AND DEREK RENCHER

Another young man, brought up in Peru, where he saw Anna Pavlova, came to London in his teens to work in the City. It was during the early 1920's. He had no money at all but somehow began to dance and, against all the rules, became one of the two greatest choreographers of our time. He is Frederick Ashton. The other, born in the same year, is George Balanchine—they counterbalance each other.

Ashton has a way of using dance so that it appears to be the only natural form of communication; his movements are often more expressive than words. And he penetrates the depths of human nature, exposing all its grandeur and pettiness with an understanding that has no malice. His choreography, sometimes deceptively simple, sometimes very complicated, does not try to push technique into unexplored regions, setting a new style in classical dance. Ashton follows the great Russian masters Ivanov and Fokine, he worships the genius of the immortal Pavlova and Karsavina, and above all he loves and respects the formal order of Petipa—but Ashton has more heart. He is the most human human being, and that is what makes the laughter and tears of timeless theatre.

One cannot pinpoint a typical Ashton ballet because each one is sufficient unto itself and his range is apparently boundless. Yet every work costs him a tremendous effort of

ASHTON AS KOSTCHEI IN *THE FIREBIRD*

soul in a long search for theme and music that will fire his inspiration. Once they are found he immerses himself in the music until he has absorbed it and it becomes movement. The movements are so much a part of the music that they look inevitable—as though they could not possibly be otherwise.

Among British contributions to the total picture of dance, apart from Scottish dance steps, which are easily identifiable in ballet technique, is a belief in modern three-act dramatic ballets, which, outside the Soviet-oriented areas, have so far been almost exclusively the work of British-reared choreographers, starting with the top three, Ashton, John Cranko, and Kenneth MacMillan. These ballets seem essential to theatre dance as a whole because they stretch the artist's interpretive powers to the limit in sustaining long roles. Also, when too much emphasis is put on technique alone, dancers are replaceable by younger legs and feet, before they ever have time to develop mature artistry. Scenic design,

THE SLEEPING BEAUTY WITH FONTEYN AND HELPMANN, NEW YORK, 1949

too, and all the resources of theatre are more thoroughly exercised in three-act ballets. If these things are ignored to excess, the art will retrogress even as it advances in other ways on its long journey from generation to generation far into the future.

If I should be teaching when I am eighty-one, which would not be surprising, as it has been the pattern for so many ballerinas in the past, it will be the year 2000 and my pupils will have a direct link, through Kschessinskaya and Preobrajenskaya, who taught me, back to 1900—even further, to 1890 and the first *Sleeping Beauty*. In that year Kschessinskaya graduated from the Maryinsky school in St. Petersburg and Preobrajenskaya was a junior member of the corps de ballet. When Preobrajenskaya was fourteen, Marie Taglioni died, and Marie as a young ballerina danced a minuet with seventy-five-year-old Auguste Vestris at a Paris gala in 1835. Vestris was born in 1760, the year John Weaver died, and Weaver was born in 1673, only one year after the first performance at the Académie Royale de Musique—otherwise known as the Paris Opera.

So in a few short steps we are back to Louis XIV and the beginning of ballet as a theatre art. It seems likely that the traditions will continue along basically the same lines, handed down from mature artist to eager pupil, gaining and losing nuances on the way. And it seems likely that the pattern for centres of new creation will shift, as it has always done, depending on the geographical placement of great ballet master–choreographers. The new inspiration will erupt in one place in a burst of energy, build to a peak, consolidate, lose pace, and sooner or later start up again elsewhere.

The only thing I can imagine that might kill off the whole process would be if every dance activity in every country were to be entirely state-controlled, or if no composer ever composed for dance again. History shows that dance thrives on challenge; new trends that keep its blood circulating appear at random in any part of the world where artists go to pursue their own individual muse, usually at some cost to themselves. Of course, a certain amount of organization and economic assistance is necessary, and some facilities wherein the new dance can be created and the new dances produced, but the more I see, the more I am sure that it is not the new buildings and ideal classrooms that will give the world its future stars; rather the reverse, it is the imaginative creators, wherever they appear, who give life to the theatres and studios in which they work. In other words, first find your creative genius, the rest will follow.

At the present time the height of dance activity is in America, but how long it will remain there and where it will settle next are matters for conjecture. Logically it should go

VENEZUELA

INDONESIA

BALI

UNITED STATES

to South America first, because that is a part of the world so rich in folk dance and so bursting with dancers that it is hard to understand why it has not yet become the world's centre. Latin Americans are dance-lovers by nature—millions of them forget everything else for three days and nights of each year to dance their way through Carnival without stopping for breath—yet, when it comes to organized theatre ballet, they are in the doldrums, and for no better reason than that it is as difficult for them to be organized as it is easy for them to dance. Another difficulty is that the enormous pool of talent is spread over so many different countries, making it harder for one centre to attract all the best elements.

In the meantime, the Far East may well get ahead, for Japan has already produced a generation of dancers to be reckoned with, and it may not be long before its Oriental culture finds expression in Western dance forms. The Chinese ballet is currently a few paces behind Japan. When it has more time and more help to advance, it will be able to draw on a wonderful store of theatre tradition and varied national dances to create a true Chinese style. India, with its rich and ancient heritage, and ramifications in the Near and Far East, finds it a struggle to preserve what it has. Uday Shankar had a vision of creating a modern theatre art mixing Indian and ballet traditions; he worked closely with Anna Pavlova and was famous in Europe and America, but he died in India in 1978 extremely poor and out of touch with all except a few loyal supporters. Ram Gopal carried on the ideas of Shankar, but there has not yet been enough support from India to encourage these projects.

Australia's aboriginal culture is a web of fascinating legends, magical and mysterious, but the most significant dances are integrated into tribal rites inaccessible to outsiders. Robert Helpmann has used aboriginal and national themes in the Australian Ballet; otherwise it is oriented to current classical and modern pieces.

In the long run, the continent that must surely affect dance more than any other is Africa, because Africans have so much dancing in their bodies. The African neck and limbs and joints have a different set to them, they produce a different line, and African dancers are able to submerge themselves in their dance with a curiously relaxed intensity unlike the more feverish concentration of other peoples. When the full power of indigenous dancing is ever put to the the service of an African genius of theatre art—a choreographer, poet, musician, and director like the ballet masters of old—there could be a stupendous outburst of vitality, rhythm, drama, and beauty that will sweep dance along like a mountain river in spring. A new magic will be born out of the most ancient of all, in that great continent where animals move with a wild and powerful grace and dancers are possessed by the gods.

SOUTH AFRICA

AMERICAN SOUTHWEST

BRAZIL

JAPAN

Some of the credits have been abbreviated as follows:

C.S.D.F: Collection Stravinsky-Diaghilev Foundation
Man.C.: The Mansell Collection
MCNY: Theatre and Music Collection of the Museum of the City of New York
NYPL: Dance Collection; The New York Public Library at Lincoln Center; Astor, Lenox and Tilden Foundations
Pavlova: Anna Pavlova, by Victor Dandré (London: Cassell & Co., Ltd., 1932)
R.M. & J.M.: Raymond Mander and Joe Mitchenson Theatre Collection
RTHPL: Radio Times Hulton Picture Library
Tchaikovsky: Tchaikovsky and the Ballet Theatre of His Time, by Yurii Slonimski (Moscow, 1956)
Th.M.: Theatre Museum, London
200 Years: 200 Years of the Leningrad State Choreographic School, 1738–1938, by Boris Oglebsky (Moscow)
V. & A.: Courtesy of the Victoria and Albert Museum, London

A

B

C

C

A NOTE ON THE GRAPHICS

The text of this book was set in the film version of Bulmer, a replica of a type face designed and cut by William Martin about 1790 for William Bulmer (1757-1830) of London. As head of the Shakespeare Press, Bulmer was one of the most successful and distinguished printers of his time. Martin employed as models for the Bulmer face the sharp and fine letter-forms of John Baskerville as well as those of Italian and French printers, especially Bodoni and Didot.

This book was photocomposed by New England Typographic Service, Inc., Bloomfield, Connecticut; printed in five colors and bound by the Kingsport Press, Kingsport, Tennessee.

R. D. Scudellari directed the graphics.
Sara Eisenman designed the layout of the book.
Ellen McNeilly directed the production and manufacturing.
Neal T. Jones and Nancy Clements supervised the manuscript and proofs.

Calligraphy by Gun Larson